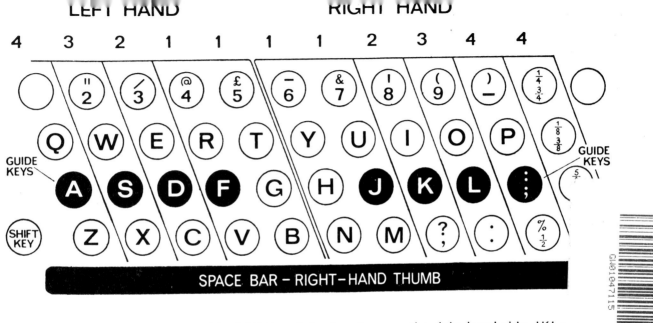

The four keys on the left-hand side A S D F and the four keys on the right-hand side J K L ; "home keys". These are the resting places over which the four fingers of the left and righ must remain, except when it is necessary to remove a finger in order to strike a key. After the key the finger must be returned immediately to its correct position.

CUT ALONG THIS LINE

PRACTICAL TYPEWRITING
Made Simple

The Made Simple Series
has been created
especially for self-education
but can equally well
be used as
an aid to group study.
However complex the subject,
the reader is taken
step by step,
clearly and methodically,
through the course. Each volume
has been prepared by experts,
taking account of
modern educational requirements,
to ensure the most
effective way of
acquiring knowledge.

In the same series

- Accounting
- Acting and Stagecraft
- Additional Mathematics
- Administration in Business
- Advertising
- Anthropology
- Applied Economics
- Applied Mathematics
- Applied Mechanics
- Art Appreciation
- Art of Speaking
- Art of Writing
- Biology
- Book-keeping
- Britain and the European Community
- British Constitution
- Business and Administrative Organisation
- Business Calculations
- Business Economics
- Business Law
- Business Statistics and Accounting
- Calculus
- Chemistry
- Childcare
- Commerce
- Company Law
- Company Practice
- Computer Programming
- Computers and Microprocessors
- Cookery
- Cost and Management Accounting
- Data Processing
- Economic History
- Economic and Social Geography
- Economics
- Effective Communication
- Electricity
- Electronic Computers
- Electronics
- English
- English Literature
- Financial Management
- French
- Geology
- German
- Housing, Tenancy and Planning Law
- Human Anatomy
- Human Biology
- Italian
- Journalism
- Latin
- Law
- Management
- Marketing
- Mathematics
- Metalwork
- Modern Biology
- Modern Electronics
- Modern European History
- Modern Mathematics
- Modern World Affairs
- Money and Banking
- Music
- New Mathematics
- Office Practice
- Office Administration
- Organic Chemistry
- Personnel Management
- Philosophy
- Photography
- Physical Geography
- Physics
- Practical Typewriting
- Psychiatry
- Psychology
- Public Relations
- Public Sector Economics
- Rapid Reading
- Religious Studies
- Russian
- Salesmanship
- Secretarial Practice
- Social Services
- Sociology
- Spanish
- Statistics
- Technology
- Teeline Shorthand
- Twentieth-Century British History
- Typing
- Woodwork

PRACTICAL TYPEWRITING
Made Simple

Margaret Davis, MBIM

Made Simple Books
HEINEMANN : London

Copyright © 1981 M. Davis
All rights reserved, including the right
of reproduction in whole or in part
in any form whatsoever

Printed and bound in Great Britain
by Richard Clay (The Chaucer Press), Ltd., Bungay, Suffolk
for the publishers William Heinemann Ltd.,
10 Upper Grosvenor Street, London W1X 9PA

First edition, December 1981
Second edition, May 1984

This book is sold subject to the
condition that it shall not, by
way of trade or otherwise, be lent,
re-sold, hired out, or otherwise
circulated without the publisher's
prior consent in any form of binding
or cover other than that in which it is
published and without a similar condition
including this condition being imposed
on the subsequent purchaser

British Library Cataloguing in Publication Data

Davis, Margaret, *1912-*
  Practical typewriting made simple.—(Made
  simple books, ISSN 0265-0541)
  1. Typewriting
  I. Title   II. Series
  652.3   Z49

ISBN 0-434-98465-5

Editorial: Robert Postema
Production: Priscilla da Cunha, Martin Corteel
Typed examples: Julie Broughton
Cover illustration: Keith Pointing

Foreword

Despite numerous developments the typewriter is still indispensable as a means of communication both in business and in private life. This book has been planned especially for the beginner, using as simple an approach as is compatible with the achievement of a good standard. The exercises are so graduated that any student who attains a reasonable degree of accuracy in each of them before proceeding to the next will have no difficulty in becoming a proficient typist. The design of the book enables it to be propped upright, thereby enabling the student to practise the exercises with minimal strain. Two charts of the typewriter keyboard are printed at the beginning of the book. One should be cut out and placed upright beside the typewriter during most of the course—until the keyboard is thoroughly mastered; the other can be kept as a spare.

Although *Practical Typewriting* is written so that it can be used for self-study by anyone who is interested in acquiring mastery of this essential skill, it can also be used with advantage by the teacher in the classroom. It will serve as an excellent introductory course for anyone working for specific typewriting examinations, such as those set by the Royal Society of Arts or for the secretarial element of a business study degree (which includes typewriting). Much of the instruction in the book is given in the exercises so that the student can read, type and learn simultaneously. Beginners will be surprised at the speed with which they will be able to master the skill of accurate typewriting through the method used in this book.

Margaret Davis
*Formerly Head of Department
of Secretarial Studies, City
of London Polytechnic*

Contents

Foreword	5
Typewriter: operative parts	10
Correct operating position	10
Paper sizes	12
Preparing to type	13
Check the paper guide	13
Set the line space regulator	13
Margin stops	13
Insert paper	14
Carriage return	14
Setting out work	14
Space bar	14
Operating the machine	14
Mastering the keyboard	15
Electric typewriters	15
Learning to type	16
Home keys	16
R U keys	18
E I keys	18
Capital letters	18
Full stop	19
O W keys	20
Q P keys	20
T Y keys	20
B N keys	21
V M keys	22
C , keys	22
: ? % keys	23
Punctuation rules	24
X key	24
Z ½ keys	25
Figures	26
4 and 7 keys	26
5 and 6 keys	27
3 and 8 keys	28
2 and 9 keys	28
" key (quotation mark/inverted comma)	31

CONTENTS

/ ' keys (slant and apostrophe)	31
@ & keys (at, ampersand)	32
£ _ keys (pound sign and underscore)	33
Back spacer	33
(and) keys (parentheses)	34
- (hyphen/dash)	35
Letters	36
Lay-out of letters	39
Semi-block form	41
Indented form	42
Fully blocked form	43
Letters for typing practice	47
Meetings: agendas and minutes	58
Reducing errors and increasing your speed	63
Word frequency	64
Tabulation	67
Roman numerals	75
Speed development	77
Typing legal documents	85
Will	86
Conveyance	87
Correcting errors	88
Fractions	92
Correction signs	92
Examination papers	96

SUPPLEMENTS

1. Abbreviations	115
2. Addressing correspondence	117
3. Addressing envelopes	119
4. Capitals	121
5. Combination characters	122
6. Division of words at line-ends	124
7. Errors to be avoided	125
8. Metrication	127
9. Modes of address	128
10. Numbers	130
11. Punctuation	131
12. Punctuation rules	133
13. Reference books	134

CONTENTS

14. Reprography — 136
    Stencil duplicating — 136
    Spirit duplicating — 137
15. Some spelling rules — 138
16. Typewriting paper — 140
17. Typing sums of money — 141
18. Words and figures — 142
19. Word processors — 143
20. Shorthand — 144

TYPEWRITER: OPERATIVE PARTS

All typewriters are similar in design but the names of their parts may vary somewhat from machine to machine even when the function is the same. For this reason, the exact locations of the parts of the typewriter illustrated in Fig. 1 may be slightly different from those on your typewriter. Extra parts that are special to your typewriter can be identified by reference to the booklet supplied by the manufacturer. These booklets are very helpful because all the contents are directed to the operation of the machine in question.

There are five main parts of a typewriter:

Carriage: The upper part of the machine which travels from right to left when a key or the space bar is struck. The carriage holds the platen around which the paper is held in position for typing.

Mainspring: The movement of the carriage is provided by an adjustable coiled spring.

Type basket: Contains the typebars to which are fixed the metal types.

Ribbon mechanism: The type strikes the ribbon and the ribbon forms the impression on the paper. The movement of the ribbon is controlled by the mechanism.

Keyboard: There are four rows each containing about 12 keys. At the base of the keyboard is the space bar.

CORRECT OPERATING POSITION

1. Sit erect, both feet on the floor, body bent slightly forward
2. Place left-hand fingers on A S D F (the 'home keys')
3. Place right-hand fingers on J K L ; (the 'home keys')
4. Curve fingers: rest fingertips very lightly on centre of keys
5. Slant hands upwards from the wrists
6. Keep elbows close to your sides

1. Margins Left/Right
2. Carriage End Covers
3. Carriage Release
4. Paper Guide Scale
5. Paper Guide
6. Line Space Selector
7. Variable Spacer
8. Platen Knob
9. Paper Bail
10. Card Holder
11. Ribbon Reverse
12. Ribbon Release
13. Carriage Return Lever
14. Tab Clear Key
15. Back Space Key
16. Shift Lock
17. Left/Right Shift Key
18. Paper Table
19. Paper Bail Scale
20. Paper Release Lever
21. Ribbon Carrier
22. Ribbon Colour & Stencil Control
23. Ribbon Selector
24. Margin Release
25. Tab Set Key
26. Tabulator Bar
27. Space Bar

Fig. 1. The typewriter and its parts.

PAPER SIZES

The International Standards Organisation (ISO) system of paper sizes is based on a sheet of paper (A0) measuring one square metre with the smaller sizes obtained by progressive halving. Paper sizes are:

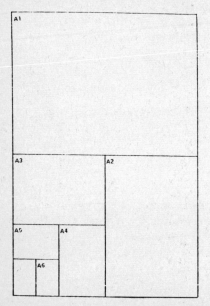

	Size in mm	Size in inches
A0	841 × 1189	33.11 × 46.81
A1	594 × 841	23.39 × 33.11
A2	420 × 594	16.54 × 23.39
A3	297 × 420	11.69 × 16.54
A4	210 × 297	8.27 × 11.69
A5	148 × 210	5.83 × 8.27
A6	105 × 148	4.13 × 5.83

Fig. 2. ISO standard paper sizes.

PREPARING TO TYPE

Place your book on the right-hand side of the machine. Place your fingers on the home keys (see page 10).
Now check your posture:

1. Hold your head erect, facing the book.
2. Shoulders back and relaxed.
3. Sit erect with body sloping slightly forward from the hips.
4. Hands, close together, flat across the backs. Fingers curved.
5. Place feet slightly apart, braced firmly on the floor. Do not cross your legs.

Check the paper guide

Adjust paper guide so that the edge of the paper will be inserted at 0 on the scale.

Set the line space regulator

The line space regulator controls the space between typed lines.

Margin stops

Margins are usually set so that the left-hand margin is $1\frac{1}{2}$ inches (or 4 cm) and the right-hand margin 1 inch (or $2\frac{1}{2}$ cm) from the edge of the paper.
The margin stops on machines are generally found in three variations:

1. At the back of the paper rest, controlled by levers.
2. At the back of the paper rest, controlled by hand.
3. At the front, controlled by hand.

Insert paper

Pull the paper bail towards you; if it will not pull forward on your machine, lift the bail upright. Insert paper in machine. The left hand turns the cylinder knob to wind the paper into the machine. Use the paper release lever to straighten the paper.

Carriage return

To return the carriage for a new line, use the carriage return lever. Use a quick sweep of the left hand and forearm to the right, returning fingers to the home keys immediately. On an electric machine the carriage is returned by striking the return key at the right-hand side of the keyboard. This key is struck with the little finger.

Setting out work

With a ruler, measure 5 inches on the typing line scale. This is the numbered scale indicating the length of line that can be typed. If 5 inches covers 50 spaces, your machine has Pica type (10 spaces to the inch). If 5 inches covers 60 spaces, your machine has Elite type (12 spaces to the inch). Six lines of typing down the page in either Pica or Elite type cover 1 inch.

Space bar

Spaces are made by striking the space bar, at the bottom of the keyboard, with the side of the right thumb—sharply. The left thumb does no work; curve it slightly under the first finger.

OPERATING THE MACHINE

Strike each key lightly but firmly and evenly with the fingertip. As you strike each key the carriage will automatically move the width of the character from right to left. When a word is complete, strike the space bar smartly with the right-hand thumb to obtain a space after the word. When you approach the end of a line a bell will ring, after which you may finish a short word or hyphenate a long one. To start a new line, return the carriage using the carriage return lever. Use the left hand, palm downwards, and move the carriage quickly to the right by striking the lever smartly. When the carriage is returned, all the fingers of the left hand must immediately return to their home keys.

MASTERING THE KEYBOARD

The learning of the keyboard starts with the 'home keys'. The home keys are the keys on which the fingers rest and from which the other keys are located. In the following pages we will cover the keyboard fairly quickly and then consolidate, by further practice, using the whole keyboard. Do not worry in the early stages if you make mistakes; the important thing is that you use the correct fingers and with practice you will find that striking the correct keys becomes automatic.

Electric typewriters

Electric typewriters are undoubtedly superior to manuals in several important respects, and it is a pity that the fatigue aspect is overstressed and more important advantages overlooked. The following are some of the advantages:

1. Uniformity of impression, regardless of the typist's touch.
2. More carbon copies can be typed.
3. Common faults are eliminated in electric typing, e.g. capital letters out of alignment, dropped lower case characters.

4. The electric machine's type provides a sharp, even striking of the keys so that it is easier to produce good quality stencils and masters for other reprographic processes.
5. On some of the more expensive electric machines sophisticated devices are included, such as proportional spacing and interchangeable type.

LEARNING TO TYPE

HOME KEYS

Type f with the left first finger and j with the right first finger. Type fj four or five times. Then type the home keys for the left-hand fdsa and the home keys for the right-hand jkl; three times. Locate the carriage return and return the carriage as directed.

Fig. 3. The home keys.

Type the lines below with a space between the two-letter groups. Hit the space bar with a quick inward movement of the right thumb.

```
ff jj ff jj dd kk dd kk ss ll ss ll aa ;; aa ;;
```

Now type the letters h and g (use j and f fingers respectively)

```
hh hj aa ha ha ss has dd had had ll lad
gg fg aa la la gg lag ss sag sag ff fag
```

Type the following lines until you feel that you have mastered the keys so far:

```
as ask as has ad had as ask as has ad had
all all hall all hall fall fall hall fall hall all
a lad had a fall; dad has hash; a lad has a dash;
a lad had a dash; dad had a dash; a lad had a fall;
ask a lass; dad had a fall; a lass had a lash;
```

New keys: r u

r is struck by the f finger,
u is struck by the j finger.
Find the keys on the chart; then locate the keys on the keyboard.

Type the following lines until you feel you have mastered the new keys:

```
full fluff dull dusk lush husk huff duff gull dull
far rag hard drag lard jar hark rush ruff rusk lurk
```

New keys: e i

e is struck by the d finger,
i is struck by the k finger.

Type the following words until you feel you have mastered the new keys:

```
did rid dud reel deal keel gear heel heal seal kill sill will lid
```

CAPITAL LETTERS

To type a capital letter depress the shift key with the little finger, holding it down until you have struck the key.

There are two shift keys; one on the right of the keyboard and the other on the left. When striking a key with the left hand, use the right-hand shift key; when striking a key with the right hand, use the left-hand shift key.

Type the following sentences until you feel you have mastered the words and the technique of using the shift key:

He has led us: He had used a desk: Sir used a desk:

She used a desk: He had a fall: She had a fall:

A desk fell: He fed a duke: She fed a duke:

THE FULL STOP

Find the full stop on the chart, then find the key on the keyboard. Strike the key with your right third finger (the l finger). After a full stop, strike the space bar twice.

Type the following sentences until you feel you have mastered them:

She had a fall. He had a fall. She was sad. He was sad. She was dull.

He was dull. Dull was he. Dull she was. He used a sled. She used a sled.

She had a dull sale. He had a dull sale. She was frail. He was frail.

A rail fell. Did he fall. Did she fall. She did fall. He did fall.

New keys: o w

o is struck by the l finger,
w is struck by the s finger.

Type the following until you feel you have mastered the new keys:

```
Will he go.  Will she go.  Will she fall.  Will he fall.  She had a doll
He had a wire.  Will he kill.  He will kill.  He will fall.  She will fall.
```

New keys: q p

q is struck by the a finger,
p is struck by the ; finger.

Type the following until you feel you have mastered the new keys:

```
quail pail pale queue pile pole roll pru pip pop
She had a quail.  He had a quail.  A quail she had.
A pile of quail.  She was pale.  He was pale.
```

New keys: t y

t is struck by the f finger,
y is struck by the j finger.

Type the following until you feel you have mastered the new keys:

```
girt hurt dirt your year you yet yolk they whey whet the there their
They were there.  She was there.  He was there.  The year was old.
Where were they.  They were here.  Who was there.  He was there.
The wood was dry.  The tour was dull.  He was dull.  She was dull.
```

New keys: b n

b is struck with the f finger,
n is struck with the j finger.

Type the following until you feel you have mastered the new keys:

```
be been bred bread Betty bought bough brought butter sudden suddenly
blade bled blood brood night nigh naught naughty bluff narrow
They were narrow streets.  The streets were bloody.  Suddenly the
streets were bloody.  The narrow streets had narrow houses.
The houses were high and nigh to the street.
```

New keys: v m

v is struck with the f finger,
m is struck with the j finger.

Type the following until you feel you have mastered the new keys:

```
vin vine wove mime most vast more home over give gave have ham
The vine was vast.  The home was vast.  Most of the vine was over
the house.  He gave him the grapes from the vine.
```

<u>Typing Practice</u>

If you devote a part of your leisure to improve your typing, you will soon be a skilful typist.
It is only by trying that you will master any skill.
I hope you feel that you have made some progress with the keyboard.

New keys: c ,

c is struck with the d finger,
, is struck with the k finger.

Strike the comma lightly. Leave one space after a comma.

Type the following until you feel you have mastered the new keys:

```
Can, Candid, Close, choose, could, cash, cheque, complete, charge,
cane, camp, certain, clerk, account.
```

New keys: ? % : (question mark, percentage and colon)

? is struck with the k finger using the left shift key,
% is struck with the ; finger using the left shift key,
: is struck with the ; finger using the left shift key.

Type the following:

```
How much?  How many?  Can you do the work?  When would you like to come?
How big is the house?  How large is the room?  How do you know?
```

```
During this month we will give you a % discount on all goods.
If your bills are paid promptly we will allow a % discount.
All our goods will be reduced by a % during the sale.
```

Would you like a % reduction in the cost of living?

Your reduction will be on cotton goods. Does this attract you?

The number of pupils is:

You should strike the keys evenly:

The poster reads: Do not smoke.

The poster reads: Do not walk on the grass.

Type the following:

PUNCTUATION RULES

Space once after: comma, semicolon and colon

Space twice after: full stop, question mark at the end of a sentence

Space once after: full stop following an abbreviation.

New key: x

x is struck with the s finger,
Review the full stop—struck by the l finger.

six etc., fix mix exceed expect expert examine tax lax extreme
mixture explosive experiment experience secret

Typing practice

Touch typing is easy to learn if you have enough confidence to rely
on your fingers resting on the right keys. Do not be tempted to look
at the paper after striking each key. You will find that your
confidence will increase the more you rely on your ability to make
the right reaches for the keys.

New keys: z and $\frac{1}{2}$

z is struck with the a finger,
$\frac{1}{2}$ is struck with the ; finger.

Type the following until you feel you have mastered the new keys:

;½;½;½;½ zest zere ;½;½ dizzy blaze ;½; size lazy zebra zoo boxes ;½;½;½;

The tall lazy man pirouetted dizzily to the drum.

The pale queen had a supper party at the zoo with sixty chimps.

If you work with zeal and zest you will soon be a success.

You must realize that poor work is a waste of time. Try to be exact.

Touch typing is easy to learn. All you need is the will to learn. The lessons in this book do the rest for you; they make touch typing easy for you to learn.

FIGURES

The top line of the typewriter is made up of figures and signs. The positions of the figures vary on different makes of machine. Some machines have the figures 1 and 0 on the top line, other machines start the top row with the figure 2 and end with 9, omitting the figures 1 and 0. Therefore when learning to type, it is easier to use the small letter l for the figure 1, and the capital letter O for nought. The letters l and O are standard on all machines.

New keys: 4 and 7

Start the top row by learning the reach for figures 4 and 7:

4 is struck with the f finger,
7 is struck with the j finger.

Practise the following line until you feel you have mastered the reaches:

```
f4f r4r j7j u7u f4f r4r j7j u7u f7mf4v f4v f4b j7n
```

Strike small l for the number one, and large O for nought:

```
101; 104; 107; 10; 100; March 1; April 4; April 14; March 7; March 17, 1014;

Add together the sum of 11 and 7 and 4 and 1 and 10 and 1470
```

New keys: 5 and 6

5 is struck by the r finger,
6 is struck by the j finger.

Type the following:

```
f5f f5f j6j j6j f5v j6m j6n f5b

The market was situated at 56 High Street, the 5th turning on the left.
There were 56 stalls in the market.
```

New keys: 3 and 8

3 is struck by the d finger,
8 is struck by the k finger.

Type the following:

```
d3d  k8k  d3d  k8k  d3d  k8k  131  311  300  301  18  181  180  183  383  813
```

New keys: 2 and 9

2 is struck by the s finger,
9 is struck by the l finger.

Type the following:

```
s2s  s2s  191  191  s2s  191

Sell 2 bags of coffee.  Buy 9 bags of coffee.

Take 2 bags of coffee and give them to the 9 people.

There are 212 passengers on the ship.

About 2 houses out of every 9 houses are leasehold.

Leasehold can be for 99 years or 999 years.
```

Practise using all the figures until you feel you have mastered the figure keys:

The train crashed and 200 people were injured.
In the school there were 20 boys but only 12 girls.

The school had an average attendance of 332 pupils.
23 girls in the school wanted to learn to type.
There were only 13 typewriters in the school.

A gross is 12 multiplied by 12 which equals 144.
The cricket match was played on the 14th of June.
The playing fields consisted of 14 acres of land.

The shop sold 5 different items.
On most days 500 people used the shop.
The customer ordered 5 tonnes of coal.

The holiday was enjoyed by 156 people.   Of that number 56 were
men, 50 women and 50 children.
The shop moved from 50 High Street to 60 High Street.
The bus company decided to run 66 more buses in the city centre.

My telephone is being installed on the 7th of this month.
I applied for a telephone on the 17th of last month.
When I bought 7 apples I found that 2 of them were bad.

I am going on holiday on the 8th of next month.
The journey will be over 800 miles.
There will be 180 people on the holiday.
Residents of this country on the holiday will be 80;
the other 100 will be from overseas.

```
Of the houses erected 19 were sold very quickly.
There were 99 houses altogether on the estate.
About 9 of the houses were not in very good positions.
These houses would be sold last.
```

New key: " (quotation mark/inverted comma)

Use the shift key for all signs above the figures. " is struck by the s finger. Use the right-hand shift key.

Type the following:

```
"I will telephone you tomorrow," said Jill.
Jill lived at "Elmtree", Lodge Avenue.
"Mr. Brown will telephone you in the morning," said Tom.
"Thank you," replied Mrs. Brown.
```

New keys: / (slant) ' (apostrophe)

/ is struck with the d finger. Use the right-hand shift key.

' is struck with the k finger. Use the left-hand shift key.

Type the following:

```
d/d k'k d/d k'k d/d k'k
The pupils left school at 8 o'clock.
He/she should sign the form.
He left his office at 7 o'clock.
He/she should register before 9 o'clock each Monday.
The railway company said they were not responsible for any
loss and/or damage.
```

New keys: @ & (at, ampersand)

@ is struck with the F finger. Use the right-hand shift key.
& is struck with the J finger. Use the left-hand shift key.

The & is called the ampersand. It is a sign for the word 'and'; it is normally used only in sentences such as those given below. The sign @ is used mainly for typing invoices. The sign for inverted commas " is used to avoid repetition of the same word in a list: they are referred to as 'ditto' marks. When listing in this way vertical alignment is essential.

Type the following:

```
F@f j@j f&f j&j

Brown & Co. have very good sale offers.

They are offering net curtain @ 90p a metre.

Questions Nos. 23, 40 & 50 should be omitted.

Read questions 3 & 4 very carefully.

Messrs. Brown & Harding.
```

New keys: £ and _ (Pound sign and underscore)

£ is struck with the f finger. Use the right-hand shift key.
_ is struck with the j finger. Use the left-hand shift key.

The character _ is called the underscore. It is used to underline words and to rule lines. To underscore a word, first type the word; then backspace to the first letter and strike the underscore key for each letter in the word. Do not underline the punctuation at the end of a line or heading.

Back spacer

The back spacer key is usually found just above the keyboard. Consult the chart supplied by the manufacturers of your machine. To use, the key is depressed; it will then move the carriage back one space.

Practise the following until you have mastered the new keys:

A driving lesson now costs £8 per hour.

A typewriter now costs about £100.

Please type these exercises <u>exactly</u> as shown.

For the attention of the <u>Finance Department</u>.

For the attention of the <u>Principal</u>.

New keys: ( ) (parenthesis)

Left parenthesis is struck with the l finger. Use left-hand shift key.
Right parenthesis is struck with the ; finger. Use left-hand shift key.

Type the following:

    1 (1 ;) 1 (1 ;) (2) (3) (4) (5) 6(6) 1 (1 ;)

Come and see me at my home, but if not convenient at my office (room 10).

(1) The price of the book (3rd edition) is £4.

(2) He inherited £7000 (seven thousand pounds).

(3) We are pleased to supply school uniforms (blue) for the girls and (brown) for the boys.

(4) I am enclosing a (prepaid) envelope.

New key: - (hyphen, dash)

- is struck with the ; finger.

It can be used as a hyphen or a dash. When used as a dash, there is a space before and after the sign. When used as a hyphen, no space is required either before or after.

;p; ;p-; ;p; ;p-; 9-room house; 20-room house; 30-room house;

One-quarter; one-half; one-eighth; one-seventh; two-sevenths;

The flowers - two dozen - have not arrived.

The butter was guaranteed pure - no preservatives.

LETTERS

The parts of a letter (see page 37):

1. **Reference:** If the printed heading does not contain a special position for the insertion of the reference then it is usually placed in the left-hand corner, two or three lines below the printed heading, in line with the left-hand margin and on the same line as the date.
2. **Date:** This is typed in the top right-hand corner (except when the fully blocked method is used), two or three lines below the printed heading. Punctuation is now usually omitted from the date—i.e. 17 April 1985—but different styles are permitted.
3. **Inside name and address:** The name and address are typed in the top left-hand corner, always in single line spacing. In block letters and semi-block, all lines begin at the left-hand margin. In personal letters it is customary to place the name and address of the addressee at the foot of the first page of the letter.
4. **Salutation:** The opening words in a letter are known as the 'salutation' and the forms used in business are:

Dear Sir, Dear Sirs, Dear Mr. Brown, Dear Madam, Dear Mrs. Brown

In addressing government or official bodies the forms generally used are:

Sir, Sirs

The salutation is typed at the left-hand margin three lines below the last line of the name and address.

(1) Ref: MD/ES **(2)** Date

(3) Mr. D. Brownlee,
67 Hamden Way,
Hamley, Bucks.
PA7 4UP

(4) Dear Sir,

(5) <u>Overdue Account</u>

I enclose a statement of account to the end of this month and would draw your attention to the fact that the sum of £100 is still outstanding from the previous month's statement.

(6) The total amount now outstanding on your account is in excess of £200 which sum we agreed was to be the limit of credit allowed. Therefore, I must now ask you to settle the balance owing or reluctantly the account must be closed and the balance collected through our solicitors.

(7) Yours faithfully,

(8) John Smith
Chief Accountant

(9) Enc.

Fig. 4. The parts of a letter.

5. **Subject headings:** It is sometimes found necessary to state the subject of a letter and this is given prominence by means of a heading. This heading is typed two lines below the salutation and can either be centred over the writing line or begin at the left-hand margin. Use the underscore key and shift lock to underline the heading. A full stop is not necessary at the end of a heading.
6. **Body of the letter:** The subject matter is contained in this part of the letter, and is arranged in paragraphs.
7. **Complimentary close:** The complimentary close should be typed two line spaces below the last line of the final paragraph of the body of the letter. The common forms of complimentary close are:

    Yours faithfully, Yours truly, Yours sincerely

    Yours faithfully or Yours truly should be used where the salutation Dear Sir is employed. Letters of a more informal nature beginning Dear Mr. . . . . . should finish with Yours sincerely.
8. **Signature:** The signature is normally handwritten—sometimes a rubber stamp impression is used. The signature is placed between the four or five lines left by the typist between the complimentary close and the designation of the writer.
9. **Enclosures:** Attention is drawn to the fact that the letter contains an enclosure by typing the word 'enclosure' either in full or in its abbreviated form 'Enc.', usually at the bottom left-hand corner of the letter. If there is more than one enclosure, then the number of enclosures should be indicated.

10. **Continuation sheets**: If a letter requires more than one page, a continuation sheet will be necessary unless both sides of the paper are used. The setting out at the top of a continuation sheet varies with the style of layout being used. A very acceptable layout for a continuation sheet and one most commonly in use is as follows:

```
S.W. Jones Esq.,              (2)                  20 October 19..
```

Type the following:

<u>LAYOUT OF LETTERS</u>

There are two main styles of setting out letters, the indented form and the blocked form. A third form is also used which is a compromise between the other two styles and is known as semi-block.

<u>The Indented Form</u>

Reference typed on the left-hand side, the date on the right. The heading is centred and the first line of each paragraph is indented. The complimentary close is typed at the middle of the writing line.

The Fully Blocked Form

<u>All</u> lines of the letter begin at the left-hand margin. In the block form there is also an increase of "open punctuation". This is the omission of punctuation from all particulars of the letter except the body of the letter, which should be punctuated in the normal way.

The Semi-Block Form

Reference typed on the left and the date on the right. No paragraph indentation. Subject headings centred on the writing line.
Complimentary close at the centre point of the writing line.

Messrs. should be used for addressing a partnership, except where the name of the company is preceded by the word 'The'.

Messrs. should not be used before the name of a limited company. A limited company is an incorporated body—a legal person, distinct from any of its members. It is generally considered that communications to a limited company should be addressed to the Secretary or other official, e.g. The General Manager.

Using A4 paper, type the following letters. Set the margins at 20 and 70. Leave 2 inches clear at the top of the paper to represent the printed letter-head. Note postcode on separate line and unpunctuated.

SEMI-BLOCK FORM

Leave 2 single line spaces—
turn up carriage three times

Leave 2 single line spaces—
turn up carriage three times

Leave 1 single line space—t.u.c. twice
Leave 1 single line space—t.u.c. twice

Leave 1 single line space—
turn up carriage twice

Leave 1 single line space—
turn up carriage twice

Leave 4 single line spaces—
turn up carriage five times

```
Our Ref. MD/ES                                    Date


Messrs. Brown & Davis,
10 Kings Road,
CHELTENHAM,
Gloucestershire.
GL21 2AE


Dear Sirs,

                    Overdue account

     It is with regret that we note that your
account with us is very much overdue, and we must
ask you to let us have a cheque within the next
seven days.

     I think you will agree that we have been very
patient in allowing you such a long credit, and if
your cheque does not reach us within the time
stated, we shall have no alternative but to place
the account in the hands of our solicitors for
collection.

                              Yours faithfully,



                              John Smith
                              Secretary
```

INDENTED FORM

Leave 2 single line spaces—
turn up carriage three times

Leave 2 single line spaces—
turn up carriage three times

Leave 1 single line space—
turn up carriage twice

Leave 1 single line space—
turn up carriage twice

Leave 1 single line space—
turn up carriage twice

Leave 4 single line spaces—
turn up carriage five times

```
Ref. VMD/ES                                    Date


Mr. R. Brown,
   20 High Street,
      Darlington.


Dear Sir,

     We have written to you several times about your
overdue account, and regret that it is necessary to
write to you again in this connection.

     As we are anxious not to incur any further
expense in the collection of this debt, we hope you
will send us your cheque in settlement of this
long overdue account within the next few days.

                         Yours faithfully,




                         John Smith
                         Secretary
```

FULLY-BLOCKED FORM

Leave 2 single line spaces—
turn up carriage three times

Leave 2 single line spaces—
turn up carriage three times

Leave 2 single line spaces—
turn up carriage three times

Leave 1 single line space—
turn up carriage twice

Leave 1 single line space—
turn up carriage twice

Leave 1 single line space—
turn up carriage twice

Leave 4 single line spaces—
turn up carriage five times

```
Date

Ref.  VMD/ES


Miss J Broughton
586 Queens Gardens
HITCHIN
Herts
HE23 4AB


Dear Miss Broughton,

This letter is an example of the fully blocked form.
The first thing you will notice is that all lines
begin at the left margin - no indentation at all.

Leave the usual spacing between paragraphs and after
the complimentary close.  This style of letter is
being increasingly used by firms.  A typist may,
during her work, type letters dictated by many
different people and it helps to avoid errors of
display if the firm has one standard layout.  The
fully blocked style also saves time.

Yours sincerely,


George Smith
Secretary
```

```
Our Ref: DS/ds                                    Date


Messrs. Gleek & Jones,
41 King Street,
CLUMPTON, Middlesex.
3AB 4CD


Dear Sirs,

                        Exhibition

     We are pleased to announce that the annual
Exhibition of our equipment will be held at our
offices in Clumpton on Monday, 1 October.

     Many new items will be included which we feel
sure will be of interest to you, and we have
pleasure in enclosing a programme together with
two invitations to attend the Exhibition and
Luncheon in the Directors' Dining Room.

     We look forward to seeing you on 1 October

                    Yours faithfully,


                    General Manager
                    Arthur Black & Sons Ltd.


Encs. 3
```

Fig. 5. The semi-block form of letter.

```
Our Ref:  GS/SA                                    Date


Mr. F. George,
   16 Green Street,
      Wickford, Essex.
         WI1 ES2


Dear Mr. George,

     Thank you for your recent letter concerning
our last consignment of timber.

     We very much regret that only half your order
was despatched.  This was due to a delay on the
part of the shipping agent in Canada, as explained
on our Delivery Note.

     However, we have now received the redwood,
and have arranged for two of our trucks to make
a special delivery to your factory on Friday
next.

                         Yours sincerely,




                         F. Johnson
                     Johnson Timber Merchant
```

Fig. 6. The indented form of letter.

Date

Ref. GK/RD

Mrs G Haynes
35 Grosvenor Mews
Kingley Sussex
SU6 7AB

Dear Madam,

<u>Winter Sale</u>

This is to remind you that our Winter Sale will commence on 1st January, and as one of our account customers you will be able to take advantage of certain special offers available on the preview day, 31st December.

Enclosed is a leaflet giving some examples of the bargains in store, but there will be many other items on offer which we feel sure you will wish to see for yourself.

Yours faithfully,

General Manager
Brown's Stores

Enc.

Fig. 7. The fully-blocked form of letter

LETTERS FOR TYPING PRACTICE

Letter to James Brown & Co., High Street, Eastbourne, today's date.
Dear Sirs, In reply to your letter of yesterday concerning the damage to your shop which occurred as the result of a street accident we have passed your remarks to our claims department. In the meantime, under the terms of your policy, it will be in order for you to place the contract for the repairs in the hands of any competent building company in your district, provided the estimate for the work is sent to us as soon as you receive it. It will be necessary to send our representative to Eastbourne to see you and to make a note of your remarks regarding the cause of the accident. We trust that you have been able to obtain the names and addresses of persons who may have witnessed the accident. Yours faithfully,

Letter to R. B. Jones, 5 Ambleside Drive, Woodford, Essex.
Dear Sir, As arranged with you on the telephone this morning, we are enclosing a proposal form in connection with the insurance of your car. If you will kindly complete and return this form to us, we shall issue a new policy. This new policy will be extended, without extra charge, to cover the points set out in your letter and agreed with us on the telephone. Yours faithfully,

Letter to W.H.B. Smith, Esq., 10 Fairland Drive, Leyton. E10 5GW
Dear Sir, We regret that it has become necessary for us to increase our prices as from the end of this month, and a revised price list is enclosed. Fuel costs in particular have influenced this decision, although in addition we are having to pay more for our raw materials. We have kept the increases as low as possible, and if the prices of fuel and raw materials are decreased we shall immediately reduce our prices in line with the prevailing levels. We hope that the trading association that has been enjoyed by our two firms will continue to our mutual advantage. Yours faithfully,

Letter to Mr. M.R. Taylor, 6 Straight Road, Coldhall, Essex. CH16 1EZ

Dear Mr. Taylor, Thank you for your letter of 23 June, asking me to clarify the rights of season ticket holders who occupy first-class accommodation on trains. I am sorry to say that you are in the wrong. Any passenger with a second-class season ticket who travels in first-class accommodation will be charged the full first-class ordinary fare for that particular journey. No allowance is made for the fact that he has a second-class season ticket. The fact that second-class accommodation is sometimes full will not be accepted as a valid reason for travelling first-class on a second-class ticket. The holder of a second-class season ticket can, if he wishes to travel first-class, pay the normal difference in fare for any specific journey before he joins the train. I hope this answers your query. Yours sincerely,

Letter to Mr. R. Harding, 30 Banner Way, Brighton, Sussex. SU6 7AB

Dear Sir, I am writing to advise you that your Increment Share Account is nearing maturity and I have pleasure in enclosing a statement of your account as at expiry of its original term. For your convenience a letter of instruction to the Society in respect of your maturing account is also enclosed. If you would care to complete and sign this and return it to me, with your passbook, in the reply-paid envelope provided, I shall arrange for your instructions to be carried out. If, alternatively, we do not hear from you, we shall assume that you would like us to renew your existing account and will arrange matters accordingly without further trouble to you. I should like to thank you for the valued support you have given the Society and hope that you will allow us to continue to be of service. Yours faithfully,

Letter to Mr. D. Grey, 35 Primrose Way, Bedwick, Essex. BW16 9HJ
Dear Sir, I was sorry to hear that you are not satisfied with the service on the Bedwick to London line. Some rush-hour trains have been very late recently but we were spared any serious industrial action. I agree with you about the latest fare increases. Unfortunately, the staggering rise in the cost of season tickets shows no sign of abating. This is, of course, a country-wide problem but our local MP has been made well aware of our feelings on this point. Yours faithfully,

Letter to J. B. Smith, Esq., 16 Bright Lane, Chelmsford, Essex. CH1 2BE

Dear Mr. Smith, I have recently rejoined Green's as Managing Director, a position I had held more than six years ago. Having worked since that time with stores in the U.S.A. and other parts of the world, it is a great pleasure to return to this fine store with its emphasis on quality merchandise and good service. Of course there have been quite a few changes, not the least being the rise in prices. This may not appear to be the time to invest in clothing, but I would like to invite you to take advantage of a special offer which I am making available to selected customers; namely, on all purchases made between now and the end of next month, I will arrange a special discount of 10%. We still offer accounts facilities in which a monthly payment of £10 will provide you with instant credit of £240 at an advantageous interest rate. Should you wish to take advantage of this offer, please bring this letter with you to the store when purchasing and if you wish to open a subscription account ask to be taken to our Accounts Department on the first floor. Yours sincerely,

Letter to Mrs. B. Jones, 77 The Rise, Amersham, Bucks. BU7 6ED
Dear Mrs. Jones, We feel that you are the type of person who appreciates good quality, value for money, and efficient service. It is for this reason that we would like to send you a copy of our new Autumn/Winter catalogue. I have a copy in front of me now. There are 980 colourful pages featuring beautiful Autumn fashions, shoes, menswear, toys, furniture, electrical goods, and lots of gift ideas. You can shop from the catalogue and you will find every price shown is the cash price, but when you want your money to go further, our 20 weeks free credit terms are a big help. You can even spread payments over 38 weeks on some more expensive items. Return this letter today in the pre-paid envelope provided, and I will send you our catalogue - absolutely free.
Yours sincerely, Home Shopping Adviser

Letter to Mrs. J. Vaughan, 15 The Brambles, Woodford, Essex. WG2 4AB

Dear Madam, I refer to your telephone call to my office today. I must point out that it is the Conservators' duty to maintain the natural aspect of the Forest and, generally speaking, it is not their policy to cut Forest grassland. Having had the area adjacent to your property inspected, I note that between the Forest and your property there are two widths of pavement and a main road and, in view of this, I do not anticipate undertaking any clearance work in that area. Yours faithfully, Forest Superintendent

Letter to Mr. G. Thompson, 5 Lennox Drive, Bexhill-on-Sea, Sussex. SU8 7GB
Dear Mr. Thompson, Thank you for your letter of yesterday, from which we were very sorry to learn of your disappointment with a recent purchase of our Superior Mild cigarettes. The cigarettes you returned have been examined by our Production Department who explain that cigarettes and filters are made separately and finally bonded together. On this occasion it is very much regretted that the adhesion was obviously not as good as it should have been. In the circumstances we are most grateful to you for drawing this matter to our attention as it enables us to strengthen our Quality Control procedures and avoid further complaints of this nature. Will you please accept, with our compliments, the 60 King Size Superior Mild cigarettes which are being sent to you. Yours sincerely,
Smokers Service Department

Sun Holidays
High Street
Amersham
Bucks
BU7 6ED

Dear Sir, I enclose my cheque for £100.00 in settlement of the balance of the sum payable for my holiday in Spain. As I am settling my account 8 weeks before departure I have deducted 10% of the cost as arranged with you for early settlement of accounts. Perhaps you will be good enough to let me know when I shall receive the documents relating to the holiday.

Yours faithfully,

Mrs J Brown
The Laurels
Brighton Sussex
SU6 7AB

Dear Madam, Today's date

<u>Health Cover</u>

We have been able to maintain subscriptions at the level fixed at the Scheme's launch in 1975; but now we are having to renew them to take account of inflation. Your subscription will not, of course, be increased until your renewal date next year.

Yours truly

MEETINGS: AGENDAS AND MINUTES

An **agenda** is a list of topics to be discussed at a meeting, and a copy should be sent well in advance of the meeting to those people required to attend, together with any relevant documents. Usually, the agenda will be attached to the Notice of the Meeting, which gives the time, date and venue. A special copy is sometimes prepared for the Chairman of the meeting, with additional information on each separate item to assist him or her in conducting the meeting, and a blank space on the right-hand side for notes.

The **minutes** are a record of what takes place at the meeting. This means recording the discussions that take place and important points raised (though not verbatim), and recording any decisions made. A note should also be made of all people present and any apologies received for absence from the meeting.

Both the agenda and the minutes are prepared and circulated by the Secretary of the meeting.

Examples of the layout for an agenda, chairman's agenda and minutes of a meeting are given below: type a copy of each.

THE CLUMPTON SPORTS AND SOCIAL CLUB
85 High Street
Clumpton   Middlesex
3AB 4CD

A meeting of the Committee of the Clumpton Sports and Social Club will be held in the Lounge Bar at the above address on Friday, 2 February, 1985, at 3.00 pm.

AGENDA

1 Apologies for absence.

2 Minutes of the last meeting.

3 Matters arising from the minutes.

4 Arrangements for next year's tennis tournament. Tennis Captain to report.

5 Election of Table-Tennis Captain following Mr. Brown's retirement from the Club.

6 Any other business.

7 Date and time of next meeting.

Caroline Jones
Secretary

Date

THE CLUMPTON SPORTS AND SOCIAL CLUB
85 High Street
CLUMPTON Middlesex
3AB 4CD

Minutes of the Committee meeting held on Friday, 2 February, 1985

Present: Mr F Smith (Chairman); Miss C Jones (Secretary);
Mrs P Charles; Mr T Gwent; Mrs H Johnson; Mrs G Lowe;
Mr C Moore; Mrs M Oldham; Miss Y Onslow; Mrs P Wilson;
Mr R Wood; Miss C Woodstock.

1 <u>Apologies</u>

   Apologies for absence were received from Mr F Gelding and
   Miss K Kent.

2 <u>Minutes</u>

   The minutes of the meeting held on 16 December, 1984, were
   approved.

3 <u>Matters Arising</u>

   Mrs Charles raised the question of a replacement for the Tennis
   Cup which was stolen last month. The Chairman reported that a
   new cup had been ordered, and it was hoped that this would be
   ready in time for this year's tournament.

4 <u>Arrangements for next year's tennis tournament</u>

   The Committee received a report from the Tennis Captain on the arrangements for next year's tournament, and it was agreed that these were entirely satisfactory.

5 <u>Election of Table Tennis Captain</u>

   The Chairman reported that two nominees had been put forward, Mrs Oldham and Mr Wood. A vote was held, and Mrs Oldham was elected the Table Tennis Captain for the coming season.

6 <u>Any Other Business</u>

   There was no other business.

7 <u>Date and time of next meeting</u>

   The Chairman informed the Committee that the next meeting would take place in one month's time, exact date, time and venue to be notified. The meeting was then closed.

Caroline Jones
Secretary

Date

THE CLUMPTON SPORTS AND SOCIAL CLUB
85 High Street
CLUMPTON Middlesex
3AB 4CD

A meeting of the Committee of the Clumpton Sports and Social Club will be held in the Lounge Bar at the above address on Friday, 2 February, 1985, at 3.00 pm.

	AGENDA	NOTES
1	Ask Miss Jones to read apologies.	1
2	Ask Miss Jones to read minutes of last meeting.	2
3	Matters arising; someone may wish to raise replacement of Tennis Tournament Cup.	3
4	Arrangements for next year's tennis tournament. Tennis Captain (Mr. Moore) to report.	4
5	Election of Table-Tennis Capt. following Mr. Brown's retirement from Club (nominations received; Mrs. Oldham and Mr. Brownlow).	5
6	Any other business.	6
7	Date and time of next meeting.	7
8	Declare meeting closed.	8

REDUCING ERRORS AND INCREASING YOUR SPEED

When you have typed for a short while you will need to analyse the errors that occur in your work. It is usually found that a typist makes recurrent mistakes; it may be that a particular letter or reach on the keyboard causes difficulty. With this in mind the following corrective drills have been included. When you have decided where your weakness lies and which keys cause the most errors, practise the words that contain those keys.

a	page absent laid passage canal banal banana and hangar garage
b	battle brook bath beating beast best bubble babble bobble
c	carrot crane carol chance lance dance occur crunch crack crockery
d	dagger drive drove drink dress desire dread guided decided
e	engine meet eyes feet there where letter here refer speed error
f	fifty feather left hefty prefer future furniture graft fortune
g	drag ground grain game gain height weight groggy bough cough
h	tough hate thought harmony hinder heavy bought shoe church through
i	image again achieve bin habit chin introduce Italy height white
j	jug juice job judge jam jolly jewel adjust jelly jig join just
k	kind joke pike fake peak rebuke kaolin kite kettle flaky beak
l	lend linger lane lunar lonely foil folly droll little cling

m	mind mend mangle muddle mode crumble common come homely amend
n	needle penny night know nun annex any many narrow noon lunch need
o	open only once oboe boat coil noun clown home moon soon two toil
p	petal happy pity puddle pony plenty keep kept prize probably peel
q	quest quad aqua quick quench question acquire quiet quite quit
r	right rain rent rut rode furry hurry grand art try radar straight
s	send sand sign song sun stir stain spend slur glassy fussy simple
t	time tan tent timber tonsil turn hurt first train tram stream
u	under turps dupe suit grumble upset tune trudge fudge puny usual
v	very verve violet vain vine curve heavy have gave save vex drive
w	way weep wind wove away awe ewe where why when week what with will
x	axe extra box fix taxation fox texture mix textbook textile exercise
y	yellow yes young type you key usually fully by sky sty stay eye
z	zest zeal crazy haze zero zinc zone zoo ozone organization zodiac

WORD FREQUENCY

Various studies have been made into the frequency with which words appear in any written matter. There have been considerable differences of opinion about the results. Words in common usage such as 'a, the, that, of, is, it, to', have been found to make up 25 per cent of normal English prose. Bearing this in mind, it is important that you compile a list of such words and practise them until they become not separate actions on a key by key basis, but a single response. A word such as 'the' should be automatic and typists should forget that they are typing three separate letters.

To increase your speed and to gain confidence in the typing of words that occur frequently in any written work, practise the following words and phrases:

```
we were where there their and then the but too yet here not reference refer
had have can cannot he she them our they your his letter
We were there.  They were there.  Their reference, your reference.  But we
were there too.  They were there too.  We cannot be there.  Their letter.
His letter.  Your letter.  We have referred to.  They have referred to.
```

The letters **t h e r w i a s** occur frequently, and you will be well advised to practise words and phrases using these letters. If you can increase your speed on all common words and phrases, your overall speed will increase dramatically.

Type the following as quickly as possible:

We regret that	Please forward to us	We are sure that you will
Last week	We regret to hear that	We hope you are satisfied
This week	We are surprised that	We are in a position to
If there is	As well as possible	Let us have your reply
I see there is	We have your letter	We shall be glad to hear that
As well as usual	Necessary attention	We will arrange the matter
That is the rule	We shall be pleased to	All parts of the world
On this subject	If there has been	We should like to hear from you
Additional cost	But if there has been	We have made enquiries
We can quote you	What do you feel	Thank you for your letter of
Yours faithfully	Which do you need	We are sure there is

TABULATION

Tabulation is typing material in columns to make it easy to read. For vertical placement of the typing on A4 size paper, subtract the number of lines required from 70 and divide this amount by 2. The answer shows the line on which the typing begins in order to centre the text on the paper. For horizontal placement count the strokes in the longest line in each column and allow six spaces between columns. The total shows the width of the tabulation. The spaces between columns will vary according to the number and width of the columns. To type the following tabulation, first read the instructions on pages 68 and 69 and then carry them out.

SCHOOL SUBJECTS

Algebra	Home Economics
Arithmetic	Hygiene
Biology	Italian
Book-keeping	Latin
Chemistry	Mechanical Drawing
Commercial Law	Music
English	Natural Science
French	Physics
Geometry	Spanish
German	Social Studies
Health Education	Trigonometry
Hebrew	Typewriting

Instructions

1. Machine adjustments:

    (*a*) Clear all tab stops.
    (*b*) Set line space gauge for single spacing.

2. Insert paper, top edge even with alignment scale.
3. Determine vertical placement for equal top and bottom margins:

    (*a*) Count the typewritten lines (13).
    (*b*) Count the blank lines between the typewritten lines (3).
    (*c*) Add these together (13 + 3 = 16); the tabulation occupies 16 lines.
    (*d*) Subtract 16 lines from 70—the total number of lines on an A4 sheet of typing paper: 16 from 70 is 54. The 54 remaining blank lines are divided in half—for equal top and bottom margins.
    (*e*) Divide 54 by 2 = 27.
    (*f*) Move the carriage to the centre of the paper: 40 (Pica); 48 (Elite).
    (*g*) Centre and type the heading 'School Subjects'. Then space down twice for the next step (horizontal placement).

4. Determine horizontal placement—for equal left and right margins:

    (*a*) For each column in the tabulation, draw a horizontal line:

    _____   _____

    (*b*) Write on the lines the number of letters and spaces in the longest line in each column:

                16   18

    _____   _____

(c) Between the lines, write the number of spaces to leave between the columns. Six spaces are equal to about a half-inch, which is an easy eye-span in reading; so let us leave six spaces:

            16   6   18
    ———————   ———————

(d) Add the figures in step (c): 16 + 6 + 18 = 40; the tabulation is 40 horizontal spaces.
(e) Move the carriage to the centre of the paper; 40 (Pica); 48 (Elite).
(f) Backspace from the centre point one-half the total number of spaces required—in this case, half of 40, which is 20. Set the left margin stop here.
(g) Tap the space bar 16 times for the longest item in the first column plus six more for the spaces between the columns, a total of 22 spaces. Set your tab stop at this point for the second column.
(h) Type the two columns across the paper, using the tabular bar or key to jump the carriage to the second column.

When a table has a title line, centre it and then drop three lines (leaving two blank spaces) before beginning the columns. If a table has several title lines, double space them and then drop three lines to the columns. Example:

```
      EXAMINATION LIST: ITEMS NEEDED FOR SHORTHAND/TYPING EXAMINATION


      Shorthand notebook                        Typing paper
      Pencils                                   Eraser
      Ruler                                     Pen
      Carbon paper                              Paper clips
      Blotting paper                            Dictionary
```

See whether you can centre vertically and horizontally the following three tabulations. Arrange each on a separate sheet.

PRINCIPAL ENGLISH CITIES

London	Sheffield
Birmingham	Manchester
Nottingham	Norwich
Leeds	Bradford
Newcastle-upon-Tyne	Bristol
Darlington	Dover
Liverpool	Coventry
Bolton	Peterborough
Southampton	Plymouth
Portsmouth	Leicester
Crewe	Derby

Centre the following tabulation on a half sheet of paper. A half sheet of A4 typing paper accommodates 35 lines from top to bottom, and is called A5 size.

TEN ENGLISH COUNTIES

Essex	Cornwall
Hertfordshire	Derbyshire
Sussex	Yorkshire
Suffolk	Lancashire
Devon	Surrey

Centre the following tabulation on a half sheet of A4 paper (A5):

PRINCIPAL RIVERS

Nile	Mackenzie
Amazon	Mekong
Mississippi-Missouri	Amur
Yangtze	Hwang Ho
Lena	Niger
Congo	Yenisey

Now practise the following tabulations:

TRATTORIA ANTONIO

MENU

Avocado cocktail
Cream of Asparagus soup
Chilled Melon

Roast Sirloin of Beef
Steak Chasseur
Saddle of Lamb
Roast Duckling Sauce Maison

THE THATCHED COTTAGE RESTAURANT

MENU

Tomato soup
Grapefruit juice

Home-made Steak and Kidney Pie
Roast Lamb
Mixed Grill
Grilled Plaice

Roast potatoes
Duchess potatoes
Petits Pois - Spring Cabbage
Cauliflower - Carrots
Braised Celery

Lemon Souffle
Blackcurrant syllabub
Fruit pie & cream
Gateaux

Coffee

Roast potatoes
Chipped potatoes
Runner beans
Peas

Ice Cream
Fruit Crumble
Peach Melba
Cheese and Biscuits

Tea or Coffee

******

WALTHAM FOREST MOTHERS' UNION

ANNUAL FETE

Saturday 22nd March 1985

2.00 pm Goldsworth Fields

P R O G R A M M E

Opening	Speech by the President	Mrs J Finch
Fancy Dress Contest	Children Aged 5-10	Judged by Mrs B Green
Cakes and Jams Competition	Entries to be donated to the Rest Assured Home for the Elderly	Judged by Miss G Smythe Mrs F Clegge
Jumble Sale and Sale of Work	Proceeds to Oxfam	Organised by Mrs J Hill
Raffle Draw	Proceeds to the Play Group	Organised by Mrs J Hill
Close	Vote of thanks to the Organisers	Mrs J Finch

ROMAN NUMERALS

I is used for 1	C is used for 100
V 5	D 500
X 10	M 1000
L 50	

A line drawn over any Roman numeral multiplies the number by one thousand:

$\overline{\text{VI}}$ represents 6,000

Questions involving the correct use of Roman numerals often occur in business and in typewriting examinations.

1 =	I	12 =	XII	40 =	XL	300 =	CCC
2 =	II	13 =	XIII	50 =	L	400 =	CD
3 =	III	14 =	XIV	60 =	LX	500 =	D
4 =	IV	15 =	XV	70 =	LXX	600 =	DC
5 =	V	16 =	XVI	80 =	LXXX	700 =	DCC
6 =	VI	17 =	XVII	90 =	XC	800 =	DCCC
7 =	VII	18 =	XVIII	100 =	C	900 =	CM
8 =	VIII	19 =	XIX	101 =	CI	1,000 =	$\overline{\text{M}}$
9 =	IX	20 =	XX	120 =	CXX	6,000 =	$\overline{\text{VI}}$
10 =	X	21 =	XXI	200 =	CC	1,000,000 =	$\overline{\overline{\text{M}}}$
11 =	XI	30 =	XXX				

Use of Roman Numerals

Study the following, then type the paragraph setting it out as shown:

1. For designation of monarchs and as class and form numbers.
   Examples: George V; Form VI; Class VIII.

2. Numbering chapters, tables or paragraphs instead of using Arabic figures.
   Examples: Chapter XIX; Table IX.

3. Very often Roman numerals are used for expressing years.
   Example: MCMLIX   (1959)

Type the following:

Joan was XV years old, Mary was XVII and Valerie was XX.
Joan was 15 years old, Mary was 17 and Valerie was 20.

The First World War lasted from MCMXIV to MCMXVIII.
The First World War lasted from 1914 to 1918.

SPEED DEVELOPMENT

Confidence is essential to success in typewriting and will help you to reach a good speed. If you are using a manual machine, correct touch is an important factor. It should be neither too heavy nor too light; if too heavy it will reduce your speed.

The following exercises contain copying matter to increase your speed. Your speed per minute can be calculated as follows:

Five strokes represent one word—divide the strokes typed by five. When the number of words has been ascertained, divide the words by the number of minutes taken to type them.

Example: 206 strokes divided by 5 = 41 words (to the nearest word). Divide 41 by the time taken to type the words. If two minutes, then divide by 2, which means that, to the nearest word, you have typed 20 words a minute.
Note: A space counts as a stroke.

```
The new dress was a deep shade of blue and just as nice as her      62

old one was.                                                        75
```

75 strokes divided by 5 = 15 words. Aim to type the sentence twice in one minute, thereby achieving a speed of 30 words a minute.

Exercises

The following exercises are for speed development. Type each paragraph first as quickly as you can, then as accurately as you can. The number of words in each paragraph is given.

Set yourself a target. In the first paragraph there are 50 words—start by allowing yourself 5 minutes to type the paragraph, thus achieving a speed of 10 words per minute. Then try typing the same paragraph in $2\frac{1}{2}$ minutes, reaching a speed of 20 wpm. Practise until you can type the paragraph in 1 minute, which will mean that you have typed it at 50 wpm.

One of the secretary's problems today is the growing number	11
of subjects of which she is expected to have some knowledge or if	24
she has not the knowledge, the ability to know where to find that	37
information. She must make herself conversant with all sources	48
of reference.	50

What is the best foundation then for a secretarial career?
First and foremost is a good standard of general education, which
must include some qualification in the use of the English language.
This good general education must be followed by a secretarial
training of a fairly high calibre. Her knowledge of shorthand and
typewriting should be of a standard that enables her to produce
accurate work.

Where a secretary has a fluent knowledge of a foreign tongue,
she will be wise to put this to good use in mastering the shorthand
of that language, but a smattering of a foreign tongue is of little
value in secretarial work. In such circumstances it is better
omitted from the training altogether.

Situations in the Office

Secretaries sometimes suffer agonies of indecision about whether or not to knock at the employer's door. There is no rule about this. Most people prefer a secretary to walk in because it is a nuisance to have to keep saying "Come in". If you are in any doubt ask your employer which he prefers.

Another embarrassing situation is the problem of whether or not to stop typing when an employer comes into the room to speak to someone else. To stop and do nothing might appear as if you wished to listen. To continue compels him to speak against a noise. I think in most circumstances it is best to stop typing, but keep busy, move away and do some filing or sorting out of papers but don't go out of the room.

Dealing with Appointments

Get the name of the caller correct even if you have
to ask them to repeat it. If the caller has called without
an appointment be careful how you put him off. Find out
whether the caller has something important he wishes to see
your employer about. If you feel it is important enough, say
that your employer has appointments all day but you will see
if he can spare the caller a few minutes.

When you show someone into your employer's room, lead
the way. Open the door and announce him by name. Stand
aside to let the visitor pass you and go out, closing the door
as soon as the caller is clear of it. Practise this. I have
seen secretaries who bumped the door against visitors in their
haste to go out after announcing them.

	Stroke	Words
It is sometimes said that high speeds are not needed	52	10
in an office but, if your speeds are high you will	103	20
have the full confidence of being able to deal easily	156	31
with the work that you have to do.	190	38

	Stroke	Words
If you wish to obtain a good post with a high salary	52	10
you should study hard and also increase your speeds in	106	21
the secretarial skills. It is sometimes said that high	161	32
speeds are not needed in an office, but if your speeds	216	43
are high you will have the full confidence of being able	272	54
to deal easily with the work that you have to do.	321	64

Every modern home now has the benefit of constant hot water. There are various ways of obtaining this modern comfort. One way is to build the boiler just behind the fireplace in one of the most used rooms, so that the fire not only keeps the room warm, but heats the water as well. This is a great advantage in the winter but is a disadvantage in the summer. This disadvantage can be overcome by installing an immersion heater for summer use.

Type and note the following:

Having practised the exercises until you have reached your target speed (without paying too much attention to accuracy), then even if it means lowering your speed, type the sentences aiming for accuracy. Do not be depressed if you find that you are making errors. The very act of striving for accuracy will sometimes cause you to make errors, but if you follow the rules and use the correct fingers, you will find that in time accuracy will not be a problem.

For further practice prepare your own short pieces of typing. The easiest way to calculate the number of words is to use a ruler. Take a piece of material typed in pica type, measure each line of type; one inch represents ten words. This is a rough guide, but will suffice for general practice. If your line span is kept to five inches, each line will represent approximately ten words and, when you have finished typing the piece, it will be easy for you to calculate how many words you have typed in the time you have set.

TYPING LEGAL DOCUMENTS

There are three stages in the preparation of a legal document:

Draft: a 'rough draft' with some words in abbreviated form and typed in treble line spacing.

Fair copy: a typed copy of the approved rough draft for submission to a solicitor or client.

Engrossment: a final copy carefully prepared without alterations for signature. Typed in double or one-and-a-half line spacing on both sides of the paper. When documents are typed in the fully blocked style, the spacing between paragraphs should be twice the amount between lines, so that the paragraphing is clearly seen.

1. If errors occur the document must be retyped. Traces of alteration might be the cause of a dispute.
2. Punctuation is usually omitted from legal documents as it is possible for punctuation to convey a doubtful meaning or for the meaning of a sentence to be altered by the addition of extra punctuation signs.
3. Words should not be divided at line ends and the right-hand margin should be made even by underscoring or ink ruling to the margin point. This eliminates any possibility of additions to the document after it has been agreed.

Legal Documents

There are various legal documents, but the rules given above apply in principle to all legal documents. The following—a will and a conveyance—are but two of such documents.

If you should be called upon to type other legal documents, you will usually be given instructions on the finer points of display, but the fundamental criteria are that there should be no ambiguity, no punctuation and each line should be dealt with so that nothing can be added.

Type the following will and conveyance on separate sheets of paper, using double line spacing.

THIS IS THE LAST WILL AND TESTAMENT of me GEORGE HAROLD BROWN of 10 High Road in the City of Birmingham----------------------------------- WHEREBY:

1. I HEREBY REVOKE all former Wills and Testamentary dispositions made by me--
2. I APPOINT Edward George Brown of 21 Greenfields in the---- County of Surrey (hereinafter called "my trustee") to be the---- executor and trustee of this my will-----------------------------
3. I BEQUEATH the following specific legacies free of any--- duties payable on and by reason of my death---------------------
(a) To my son HENRY GEORGE BROWN the sum of five thousand---- pounds--
(b) To my daughter FRANCES LILIAN BROWN the sum of five------ thousand pounds--
(c) To my wife MARY ALLISON BROWN I GIVE DEVISE AND BEQUEATH- all the residue of my property whatsoever and wheresoever------ absolutely--
IN WITNESS whereof I have hereunto set my hand this
day of   One thousand nine hundred and

SIGNED by the above-named   )
GEORGE HAROLD BROWN as his   )
last Will in the presence of   )
us both being present at the   )
same time who in his presence   )
and in the presence of each other)
have hereunder subscribed our   )
names as Witnesses   )

Note: Blanks are filled in (in ink) on execution.

THIS CONVEYANCE made the   day of   One thousand
nine hundred and
BETWEEN CHARLES SMITH of 62 High Street in the City of-
Birmingham Stock Broker and ALFRED COOK of the BRAMBLES
Ham Common in the County of Surrey Gentleman of the----
other part WITNESSETH that in the consideration of the----
sum of thirty thousand pounds now paid by the said------
ALFRED COOK to the said CHARLES SMITH in respect of the
purchase of the fee simple absolute in possession free-
from incumbrance of the property hereinafter described-
(the receipt of which sum the said CHARLES SMITH hereby
acknowledges) the said CHARLES SMITH as Beneficial----
Owner hereby conveys unto the said ALFRED COOK---------
ALL THAT messuage or dwelling house situated in and----
being No. 9 Charles Street in the City of Salford------
TO HOLD the same unto the said ALFRED COOK in fee------
simple---
IN WITNESS whereof the said CHARLES SMITH and the said-
ALFRED COOK have hereunto set their hands and seals the
day and year first above written

Signed sealed and   )
delivered by the   )
said CHARLES SMITH   )
in the presence of   )

SIGNED SEALED AND   )
DELIVERED by the   )
said ALFRED COOK   )
in the presence of   )

Type the following:

<u>CORRECTING ERRORS</u>

The object of typewriting is to produce accurate work. If errors are made, they can be corrected by means of a rubber eraser, correction paper or correcting fluid.

Correction paper consists of chemically treated strips of paper. Backspace to the letter or word to be erased, place the strip of paper over the error with the imprinted side facing you, retype the error through the strip, remove the strip and type the correct letter or word. The strip may be used many times, but the used portions must not be typed over. The strips should not be rubbed or folded.

Correcting fluid is used by painting out with the fluid the letter or word to be erased, allow to dry and then type over the space the correct letter or word.

Some modern typewriters have a special white correction cartridge fitted to them. The operation of this cartridge is made by the depression of a key; instructions for its use will be found in the maker's instructions supplied with the machine.

If you are conscious of making an error, you should correct it before going on. If the errors are not discovered until after the work has been taken from the machine, the sheet can be replaced, the erasure made, and the correction typed in with the help of the line gauge (the small scale or scales resting against the platen). The line in which the correction is to be made must be adjusted until it is flush with the line gauge. The paper is gripped between rubber rollers and it must be set free before it can be moved to the correct position. This is done by means of the paper-release lever. The paper must be moved until the characters fall exactly over the scale degrees. Some practice may be necessary before you are able to do this quickly. When the proper position for one line has been found, the rest of the lines will fall into place without further adjustment, so that other corrections on the same page can be made.

Never type the correct letter over an error without first erasing. This is called over-typing and should never be done. It is heavily penalised in typewriting examinations.

It may sometimes be necessary to make a correction that involves erasing a word containing three characters and typing in its place one containing four characters. This kind of correction is known as "half-space" correcting, and can be done with the aid of the back-spacer. The position of the back-spacer varies on different makes of typewriters. Its function is to move the carriage from right to left. When the back-spacer is depressed firmly and completely, the carriage moves from right to left one complete space. When the back-spacer is half-depressed, the carriage moves from right to left only half a space, and it is this movement that is necessary in half-space correcting. When this method of correction is used, the space before and after the new word is less than standard. Half-spacing is not recommended for examinations, but it is very useful in office work.

Typing practice

The sign - is used for both the hyphen and the dash, but it is essential to distinguish between the use of the hyphen and the dash. The hyphen is used to separate two linked words or syllables. The hyphen is also used to divide words between syllables at the end of a line. When the bell on the typewriter rings, finish the word if it is short - less than six letters. If longer, divide the word at the end of a syllable. The hyphen has no space before or after it. But when the key is used as a dash, a space before and after is required.

FRACTIONS

The position of fractions differs with the make of the typewriter. Study the position of the fractions on your machine, check with the chart the correct finger to use for each fraction. Now type the following sentences using the correct finger for each fraction:

    The book measured $5\frac{1}{2}$ x $4\frac{1}{4}$

    He inherited $\frac{3}{4}$ of his father's estate.

    A block $4\frac{3}{4}$ x $4\frac{3}{4}$ is a square.

    Add $\frac{1}{4}$, $\frac{1}{2}$, $\frac{3}{4}$ and $\frac{1}{2}$; the sum is two.

CORRECTION SIGNS

Drafts prepared for printing should be typed in double line spacing on one side of the paper. Leave margins of $1\frac{1}{2}$ inches at the top and 1 inch at the bottom. If manuscript is to be bound, leave a margin of 2 inches on the left. Use good quality paper and a black, fadeless ribbon. The following correction signs are used in the office for correcting draft letters or draft reports.

⋏	= caret sign (indicates omission)
⊙	Insert full stop at caret sign ⋏
,/	Insert comma at caret sign ⋏
'/	Insert apostrophe at caret sign (John⋏s book)
" "	Insert inverted commas at caret signs (⋏Do this,⋏ she said)
/-/	Insert hyphen at caret sign (Do not be half⋏hearted)
H	Insert dash at caret sign (I won't ⋏ I'll do it well)
(/)/	Insert brackets at caret signs ⋏I'll do it well⋏
#/	Insert space at caret sign
eq.#	Equalise the spacing
l.c./	Change Capital (upper case) letter to small (lower case)
u.c./	change from lower case to upper case
ital /	Type words underlined in *italics*
bold /	Type words underlined with a wavy line in **bold print**
caps	Type words doubly underlined in capital letters
sp caps/	Type words trebly underlined in spaced capital letters
trs/	Transpose - change the sequence or order of the letters, words, or phrases
⌀/	Delete (omit)
stet/	'Stet' = 'let it stand' Leave word(s) in ~~after all~~ (dotted line indicates word(s) to be left in)
NP/	Start new paragraph where indicated by bracket [
run on	Do not make new paragraph — Join the two paragraphs together
☐	Indent first word to point shown
⊐	Move to left
⊏	Move to right
lower	Lower
raise	Raise
‖	Straighten margin
⌒/	Take out space and close up /leave more space between lines

Fig. 8. Correction marks.

Type the following, making the corrections indicated:

A/ OFFICE MACHINES: <u>care and cleaning</u> *Caps*

If machinery is to operate satisfactorily then it must be kept clean and maintained properly. Towards the end of the guarantee, the *period* **n/** maker's agent should be contacted to examine the machine to ensure that it is in good condition before it becomes subject to normal **stet** ~~maintenance~~ charges.

Accidents continue to happen even though every attempt is made to ensure that machines are safe. Accidents are sometimes due to **trs/** careless use, sometimes to machine faults. Accumulated dirt **#/** can make a machine dangerous to the user.

Typewriters

The amount of cleaning which can be done by the typist will depend on the model and whether the machine is electric or manual. Type must be kept clean. If the type is brushed frequently with a hand brush be sure that you brush the type towards the keyboard, not inwards towards the platen and never sideways, as sideways brushing will eventually bend the type bars and spoil the alignment of the type. Before moving a typewriter the carriage should be immobilised. Never move a typewriter by holding the ends of the carriage.

Safety of Electric Typewriters

If a fault occurs which appears to be connected with the electrical parts, do not attempt to correct it. Switch off the machine, unplug the machine and seek the assistance of a trained mechanic. It is dangerous to tamper with electrical equipment. At the end of the day or when the machine is not going to be in use make sure that it is switched off at the mains switch. A machine left switched on, particularly overnight, is a serious fire risk and also it causes unnecessary war on the motor.

ROYAL SOCIETY OF ARTS EXAMINATIONS IN TYPEWRITING

RSA examinations are arranged in three stages: Stage I — Elementary; Stage II — Intermediate; Stage III — Advanced.

Four examinations in all stages are held each year. A programme, including general regulations and a list of centres, and copies of previous examination papers, may be obtained at a small cost from the Royal Society of Arts (Publications Dept.), Murray Road, Orpington, Kent, BR5 3RB.

Below you will find an example of an RSA Stage I examination paper and a Stage II speed test.

THE ROYAL SOCIETY OF ARTS EXAMINATIONS BOARD
TYPEWRITING
STAGE I (Elementary)

(TIME ALLOWED—TWO HOURS AND FIVE MINUTES)

1 The examination is in three parts:

    1.1   5 minutes   for "warming up"—practice material is printed overleaf.

    1.2   10 minutes   for reading through the examination paper; during this period you may make notes and calculations (you may mark them on the examination paper if you wish) but you must *not* begin to type until the invigilator tells you to do so.

    1.3   1 hour 50 minutes   to complete the following tasks:

        TASK 1   Article (16 *marks*)
        TASK 2   Letter with carbon copy (17 *marks*) and envelope (5 *marks*)
        TASK 3   Article (24 *marks*)
        TASK 4   Table (12 *marks*)
        TASK 5   Memorandum (16 *marks*)
        TASK 6   Form for completion (10 *marks*)

2 You may work the tasks in any order, but you should attempt all of them.

3 Start each task on a fresh sheet of paper (you may use the back of the sheet to finish the task, unless otherwise instructed).

4 Any *satisfactory* method of correcting mistakes on top and carbon copies may be used.

5 Letters and memos must be dated with the date of the examination, unless otherwise indicated.

Straight copying

The thing about the home handyman is that he is generally of the office-worker type, a clerk or a manager or a teacher - someone who works with his head most of the time, but likes to be a bit handy at weekends. The man who said that should know, for he runs a big DIY shop somewhere in the north of London.

"I had a doctor in here the other day: we get a lot of doctors. He may have been an accountant, perhaps. Anyway, he picks up this big plough plane, and I see him making little planing motions in the air with it, and then he looks up and says that it really makes him want to do a bit of planing. That happens a lot. People come wandering in, they see a nice tool or maybe the latest type of masonry drill, they have a think about it, and then they buy it, and you just know they will go home to think up a special job to do with this new purchase."

Keyboard practice
a;sldkfjghfjdksla;sldkfjghfjdksla
abc def ghi jkl mno pqr stu vwx yz.
zyx wvu tsr qpo nml kji hgf edc ba.

The concert began at 7.30 and finished at 9.25. The interval of 20 minutes was between 8.15 and 8.35. The first item lasted 10 minutes; the longest one took 50 minutes.

Task 1 (16 *marks*)

Type on plain white A4 paper.
Use double (or 1½) line-spacing

TIME BALL TOWER, BEACH STREET, DEAL, KENT

Originally this building, situated at the entrance to the Old Navy Yard, was 1 of 10 royal signal towers wh. were used to Semaphore messages to the Admiralty from the fleet at the Downs during the Napoleonic Wars. At Greenwich in 1833, the first time ball was installed to enable ships on the Thames to check their chronometers. In 1855 a similar time ball of copper, mounted on a 4.27 m (14 ft) mast, was installed on top of the tower. At 12.55 pm every day the ball was raised halfway; at 12.58 pm it reached the top of the shaft & at 1 pm it was brought down by electric current direct from Greenwich and was thus able to give correct time to ships at the downs.

This system was in operation until 1927 when it was replaced by wireless time signals. Still put to practical use, the building became Deal's Information Centre.

Task 2

(22 *marks*—*letter* 17 *marks; envelope* 5 *marks*)

Type on the headed A4 paper.
Take a carbon copy on the yellow paper.
Type an envelope.

Our ref BP/ML/rb

Richard J Page Esq
10 White Hill Close
MAIDSTONE
Kent
ME15 6BR

Dear Mr Page

LATE ARRIVAL OF THE PRAXI CHRONICLE

Thank you for your letter of 19 June, together w. your cheque for £47 wh. enables us to renew your subscription for a/ year until the end of July 1981.

further /

I am sorry to hear of the late delivery of your PRAXI CHRONICLE & I am taking the matter up with the Post Office. I am sorry too about the folding of the wrapper in wh. a recent issue was received

certainly / & I will / take this matter up with the Production
trs Manager to ensure th. the copies are (correctly folded) & th. the address is clearly shown.

I will inform you of the outcome of my enquiries as soon as I receive a reply from the
uc post office.

stet Yours ~~faithfully~~ ~~sincerely~~

B. Pearson
Subscription Manager

Task 3 (24 *marks*)

Type on plain white A4 paper.
Retain all figures shown.

WINCHESTER - ENGLAND'S ANCIENT CAPITAL

Winchester is situated 12 miles from Southampton at a point in the Itchen Valley where the Downs converge from either side. It owes much of its charm to its compactness. From the City centre it is only 15 minutes' walk into open country by the river. // One can walk to the site of an Iron Age Settlement on St Catherine's Hill; or one can follow a footpath along the river to St Cross Hospital - surely the finest mediaeval almshouse in England.

para

run on

With its Gatehouse, XIIth century church and quadrangle, in which the Brothers live, St Cross gives an idea of what the monasteries of mediaeval England must have looked like.

lc

Of the Royal Castle all that remains is the Great Hall (XIIIth century). The Hall was the meeting place of the first English Parliaments and was the scene of several famous trials, notably that of Sir Walter Raleigh, who was sentenced to death here. In the Castle Hall hangs the famous Arthurian round table, the origin of which is unknown.

RALEGH
uc

Just outside the City Wall is the College, founded in 1382, which has ever since been one of England's leading schools. The mediaeval buildings remain, and there have been some noteworthy later additions.

later l

However, the glory of Winchester today is undoubtedly the Cathedral with its vast nave, Norman transepts, magnificent altar screen and the beautiful close which surrounds it.

uc

Task 4 (12 marks)

Type on plain white A4 paper.

CAPS

Word	Synonym	Antonym
Ambiguous	Doubtful	Obvious
Boisterous	Noisy	Peaceful
Cessation	Ending	Beginning
Deference	Respect	Disrespect
Expeditious	Prompt	Slow
Gloom	Darkness	Brightness
Hopeful	Expectant	Despairing
Indifferent	Impartial	Biased
Jumble	Order	Confuse
Love	Affection	Hate
Numerous	Abundant	Scanty
Obsequious	Deferential	Independent
Foolish	Absurd	Wise
Melancholy	Depression	Gaiety

trs

Task 5 (16 *marks*)

Type on the printed A4 memorandum form.

From   RADIO CONTROLLER
To   WARD SISTER
Ref   EXT 2771

PATIENTS' REQUEST FORMS

CAPS

I enclose a number of forms in connection with our new programme "PHONE US WITH A REQUEST" which will be broadcasting as from next Friday evening at 8.15 pm.

I sh. be grateful if you will allow these forms to be distributed to all patients under your care. The completed forms can be handed in at the Ground Floor **stet** Reception Desk or posted in any of the internal post boxes located on each floor.

close up

Programmes will be on Channel 2 as follows:

Wednesday	7.30 pm	Saturday	8.00 pm
Thursday	7.30 pm	Sunday	3.00 pm
Friday	8.15 pm		

Our telephone lines will be open during all programmes for requests.

Encs

Task 6 (10 *marks*)

Complete the printed form for ~~Mr~~
Richard Jonathan Page who lives at
10 White Hill Close, Maidstone, Kent
ME15 6BR

A second card is required for ~~Mrs~~
Margaret Ann Page

Their current account number is
00296705

The title of account is
R J and Mrs M A Page

The Praxi bank branch is
Maidstone West
and the cards will be collected
Today's date
Leave the space for the signatures blank

ROYAL SOCIETY OF ARTS EXAMINATIONS BOARD
TYPEWRITING, STAGE I—SUMMER SERIES 1980

Insert the number on your answer book here

THIS FORM—FOR USE IN WORKING TASK 6—MUST BE INSERTED INSIDE THE COVER OF YOUR ANSWER BOOK AT THE CONCLUSION OF THE EXAMINATION.

PRAXIPOINT APPLICATION FORM
To: Praxi Bank Limited
Please issue a Praxipoint Card to:

First card	
Second card (joint accounts only)	
Address	

Title of Account	
Praxi Bank Branch	
Current Account No.	
Please hold the card(s) until collected *☐	
Please post the card(s) *☐	
Date	
Usual signature(s)	

*Insert an X as appropriate

THE ROYAL SOCIETY OF ARTS EXAMINATIONS BOARD

TYPEWRITING—STAGE II (Intermediate)

SPEED TEST

5 minutes allowed

As this is a speed test you are not allowed to correct any mistakes you may make; <u>a corrected speed test will not be marked.</u>

Type in single, $1\frac{1}{2}$ or double line-spacing, using blocked or indented paragraphs. You may follow the same line endings if you wish.

Any number in the text should be copied exactly: do not change words to figures or vice-versa.

The figures in the left margin are not to be typed; they indicate the lines on which specified speeds are reached.

If you finish the passage before the end of five minutes go back to the beginning and start again.

If you type to the bottom of the first side of the typing paper provided, turn it over and continue typing on the back.

In an office we depend a great deal on the aids and machines that are there to help us with our work, and it is interesting to speculate about what causes the worst chaos when something goes wrong or can not be obtained. One could argue, for instance, that an office could not go on for long without its telephones: yet many did, during the time when the operators were on strike. The facilities for postage, too, are important; but many other ingenious ways were found of getting papers from place to place when the postmen were not working.

There have been threats of power cuts from time to time, and they have in fact occurred often. One must admit that one cannot do any written office work once it gets dark on a winter afternoon, during a cut; and a great many items of electric machinery at once become quite useless for the time being.

(35 wpm) (The manual typewriter may have a longer future than we think.)

(40 wpm) The number of cups of tea and coffee that can be drunk goes down; and some unlucky workers may find themselves stuck in the lift until such time as the power comes on again.

(50 wpm) When paper is in short supply there are apt to be difficulties; though at the same time it is clear that economy in the use of existing paper stocks in one of the easiest things to achieve in times of shortage - provided of course that the telephone is still working.

(60 wpm) It seems that at the present time the thing that has the most crippling effect in the office is the sudden lack of the photocopier, when it is out of commission. The whole tempo of work has to change to meet this new situation: time has to be made for taking carbon copies; for reading matter over the phone; for taking a document round from one person to

(70 wpm) another, or getting people to come and look at it, instead of just sending them a copy of it. A meeting where everything has to be explained orally becomes much longer than one where papers have been read in advance, even if they have had to be
(80 wpm) read at quite short notice.

They say that a bad workman blames his tools, but most people would agree that it is only by having the right tools and equipment that work can be done well, without strain and fatigue. This applies to young workers as well as adults, and even to the early days of school, where it is just as important that equipment for learning and working should be suitably designed.

Figures show that the average height of school children has increased during the past 30 or so years, yet the height of school furniture has become lower. The result is that children

often have to contort themselves into awkward positions before
they can read at the distance of 250 mm which is thought suitable.
This puts great strain on the soft bones in the spine. Ailments
of the back are often found in childhood, and the most likely
(35 wpm) reason for them is bad posture caused by poorly designed furniture.

(40 wpm) A Danish surgeon travelled round his country, and searched in
vain for at least one school class that had furniture that
could be said to be adequately designed. He took photographs
of a group of young pupils, with an automatic camera, during
a four-hour examination: one picture was taken every 24 minutes.
(50 wpm) They showed that most of the pupils were bent over in unsuitable
postures because the height of their desks was too low for them.

He then invited some children to take turns to sit on a chair
which had a pivoted seat, behind a table with a pivoted top:
(60 wpm) both the table and chair could be adjusted for height. He
found that most of the children had clear ideas about what
height they preferred, and even if he altered the height himself
several times, they always moved it back to the one they liked.

(70 wpm) Some two years ago a body called the ISO (International Standards
Organisation) put forward their ideas for new standards for school
chairs and tables. One would have hoped that they would be the
same as those described above, but sad to say, they are for
(80 wpm) heights that are even lower.

© R.S.A., 1980

SUPPLEMENTS

ABBREVIATIONS

Abbreviations fall into two main groups:

(*a*) Abbreviations found in manuscripts and draft documents.
(*b*) Recognised abbreviations used in commerce.

Ampersand (&): This is used in typewriting only when it occurs in the name of a firm. It is used in the name of a firm even when this appears in the body of a letter.

e.g.; viz.; i.e.: When performing their true function as abbreviations, these are always preceded by a comma, but not followed by one.

Full stop: Recognised abbreviations are indicated by the use of a full stop, but there are certain symbols which are not strictly abbreviations, and these do not need the stop:

    £
    1st, 2nd, 3rd, etc.
    per cent
    Roman numerals

Re: This is not a preposition or an abbreviation of 'reference' or 'referring' but part of the Latin phrase *in re*. It should not be used to precede a heading or instead of 'with reference to'. If it is dictated the typist should not give it an abbreviation stop.

The following are examples of abbreviations where two letters appear close together with no separating point:

    pp.   pages
    MS.   manuscript
    MSS.   manuscripts

PRACTICAL TYPEWRITING

Notes:
(*a*) As P.S. (post-script) represents the one word *postscriptum* it seems unnecessary to separate the two letters by a point and some printers recommend the form PS.
(*b*) It is not necessary to raise the point in percentages, e.g. 6.5%, or in sums of money, e.g. £6.50.

2

ADDRESSING CORRESPONDENCE

Post Towns

These act as clearing points for a particular district and are keypoints of the postal system, specially chosen for their accessibility. The Post Town is a vital part of a postal address and should always be shown in BLOCK CAPITALS.

Postcodes

A Postcode is a group of letters and figures which represents an address in abbreviated form, as an aid to automatic sorting. Postcodes have already been issued to most towns. Details of the appropriate Postcode are sent to all addresses in each area, and all people living and working there are asked to use them as part of their normal address.

The Postcode should always appear in block capitals as the last item of information in any address.

Information about Postcodes can be obtained from Head Postmasters.

The address should include in all cases:

(*a*) Name of addressee
(*b*) Number of the house
(*c*) Name of the thoroughfare
(*d*) Name of Post Town in Block capitals
(*e*) Postcode

The use of abbreviations for county names which are not postally acceptable is liable to cause confusion and lead to delay. The county name should be shown in full unless a shortened form for it appears in the following list of postally acceptable abbreviations:

PRACTICAL TYPEWRITING

Bedfordshire	Beds.
Berkshire	Berks.
Buckinghamshire	Bucks.
Cambridgeshire	Cambs.
County Londonderry	Co. Derry
County Durham	Co. Durham
Mid Glamorgan	M. Glam.
South Glamorgan	S. Glam.
West Glamorgan	W. Glam.
Gloucestershire	Glos.
Hampshire	Hants.
Hertfordshire	Herts.
North Humberside	N. Humberside
South Humberside	S. Humberside
Lancashire	Lancs.
Leicestershire	Leics.
Lincolnshire	Lincs.
Middlesex	Middx.
West Midlands	W. Midlands
Northamptonshire	Northants.
Northumberland	Northd.
Nottinghamshire	Notts.
Oxfordshire	Oxon.
Staffordshire	Staffs.
East Sussex	E. Sussex
West Sussex	W. Sussex
Tyne and Wear	Tyne & Wear
Wiltshire	Wilts.
Worcestershire	Worcs.
North Yorkshire	N. Yorkshire
South Yorkshire	S. Yorkshire
West Yorkshire	W. Yorkshire

3

ADDRESSING ENVELOPES

1. Use double spacing for a three-line address and single line spacing for an address of four lines or more.
2. Addresses may be typed in either block or indented form.
3. Type town in BLOCK CAPITALS.
4. Postcode to be typed on a separate line and unpunctuated.
5. Type annotations such as 'Attention', 'Personal', etc., on the left top corner of the envelope.
6. Window envelopes are now widely used, thus saving the need to address envelopes.

```
CONFIDENTIAL

Mrs M Brown
27 Whitehall Road
The Meads
BOLTON
BL4 9EL
```

PRACTICAL TYPEWRITING

```
URGENT

Mr A A Lines

    20 The Broadway

        LONDON

            QC2B 6AS
```

Fig. 9. Envelope addresses.

4

CAPITALS

The modern tendency is to use lower-case letters as far as possible. The following is a summary of instances in which initial capitals are essential:

(*a*) Reference to the Deity and for all pronouns and synonyms relating thereto;
(*b*) Festivals, days and months, and special events, e.g. Christmas, Michaelmas Day, the Reformation. Note that the seasons—spring, summer, autumn and winter—do not require initial capitals.
(*c*) Compass points and names of roads and streets;
(*d*) Titles of distinction and abbreviations, e.g. Sir, M.A., O.B.E.
(*e*) Titles of books, plays, etc.
(*f*) The first letter of every line of poetry.

In ordinary literary matter, the use of a capital letter can make an important difference to the meaning:

The *Band* of H.M. Scots Guards was surrounded by a *band* of admirers.

5

COMBINATION CHARACTERS

As indicated in an earlier chapter, the keys on a typewriter for numbers and signs can vary. Therefore, a typist sometimes has to use a little ingenuity in order to obtain the sign that is required. This means using a combination of available keys to make up the sign required.

Type the following and keep it for reference, even though your present machine may have some of the characters indicated.

- ! **The exclamation mark:** Type the apostrophe and then backspace to type a full stop.
- ✱ **The asterisk:** Turn the roller back half a space, type the hyphen, backspace and type a small x. Remember to return the roller to its original position.
- ÷ **The division sign:** Type the colon first, backspace and type the hyphen.
- $ **The dollar sign:** Type a capital S and backspace before typing the slant.
- † **The dagger:** Type a capital I, backspace and type a hyphen over it.
- ‡ **The double dagger:** The dagger and the double dagger are used in literary work. Type a capital I, backspace and use the interliner to turn the roller a fraction of an inch and type another capital I slightly overlapping the first.
- ' **Feet or minutes:** Use the apostrophe.
- " **Inches or seconds:** Use quotation marks.
- - **Minus sign:** Use hyphen.
- x **Multiplication sign:** Use small x.

PRACTICAL TYPEWRITING

+ **Plus sign:** Type hyphen, backspace and move roller up slightly; type apostrophe.

§ **The section sign:** Type a capital S, backspace and use the interliner to turn the roller slightly before typing another capital S.

/ **The square bracket:** This can face either way. To type a right-facing bracket, type the slant, backspace and type the underscore. It should look like this / . Turn the roller up one whole line space and type another underscore.

_/ To type the square bracket facing left, type the underscore then the slant. Backspace and turn the roller up one whole single line space and type the underscore again.

6

DIVISION OF WORDS AT LINE-ENDS

The rules to be followed are for the most part based on the effect that the break will have on the easy reading or understanding of the typescript. Do not divide a word unless it is absolutely necessary.

Divide:

(*a*) after a prefix or before a suffix;
(*b*) where a consonant is doubled, divide between the consonants, e.g. neces-sary;
(*c*) a hyphenated word must be divided at the hyphen;
(*d*) divide words according to syllables.

Do not divide:

(*a*) words of one syllable or their plurals;
(*b*) proper names;
(*c*) sums of money;
(*d*) numbers;
(*e*) abbreviations, e.g. U.S.A.;
(*f*) the last word on a page;
(*g*) the last word in a paragraph.

It is better to have a character or two extending into the margin than to break the rules for word division or to leave a very short line. To finish a word that should not be divided at the line end, use the margin release key.

7

ERRORS TO BE AVOIDED

1. Wrong spelling;
2. Untidy erasures;
3. Irregular line spacing;
4. Incorrect punctuation;
5. Striking a correct character over an incorrect one;
6. Incorrect spacing after words or punctuation marks;
7. Incorrect division of words at line ends;
8. Piercing the paper with the full stop and other punctuation marks;
9. Uneven left-hand margin and undue irregularity in the right-hand margin;
10. Insufficient or excessive margins at the left hand, right hand, top or bottom of paper;
11. Faulty use of the shift key causing the upper case signs to be out of alignment;
12. Irregularity of striking the keys (on a manual machine) so that the letters are too heavy, too faint or do not appear at all.

Type of error	*Probable cause*	*Suggested remedy*
Omission of space or letters	Typing too fast	Slow down. Type with better control of fingers.
Too many spaces	Pushing the space bar	Strike the space bar sharply
Raised capital letters	Releasing the shift key too soon	Hold the shift key until you have struck the letter

PRACTICAL TYPEWRITING

Omitting or inserting words	Losing your place in the copy	Keep your eyes on the copy, even when returning the carriage.
Uneven left margin	Returning the carriage too slowly or too sharply	Practise returning the carriage with the same force for each line.

8

METRICATION

Rules for typing	*Reasons and examples*
(a) Symbols are the same in the plural as they are in the singular	1 m = one metre 10 m = ten metres
(b) Never put a full stop after a symbol except at the end of a sentence	They are symbols, not abbreviations
(c) Leave single space between figures and symbols	1 kg
(d) Avoid hyphenating a unit	millimetres, *not* milli-metres
(e) Use the correct case of type	kg, *not* Kg
(f) To avoid confusion write 'litre' and 'tonne' in full	91 l incorrectly written as 91l could be confused as nine hundred and eleven. The symbol for 'tonne' (t) is sometimes incorrectly used for (imperial) ton.

Note: 'ton' and 'tonne' are pronounced the same, so to avoid confusion when speaking say 'metric tonne'.

9

MODES OF ADDRESS

When writing to someone who is entitled to various combinations of letters after his name, it is important to get these letters in the correct sequence. A person must be addressed by some form of title, e.g. Sir, Captain, Mr. (or Esq.), and they should appear in this order:

1. Title
2. Orders and decorations
3. University degrees
4. Distinctions, etc.

Mnemonic to help you remember this sequence:

Conferred by Crown, University, any other.

Note: V.C. (Victoria Cross) is the most distinguished of all decorations, and precedes everything.

Example: Sir John Smith, V.C., K.C.B., D.S.O., M.A., M.P.

Titles

Miss	(complete word—no stop)
Mr.	(for mister)
Esq.	(for esquire)
Mrs.	(for mistress)
Herr	(complete word—no stop)
M.	(for monsieur)
MM.	(for messieurs)
Mlle	(for mademoiselle—no stop)
Mme	(for madame—no stop)

PRACTICAL TYPEWRITING

Esquire

The once almost universal use of this title for every man has established in some quarters the impression that the use of Mr. is considered to be impolite. There is no clear agreement as to which term should be used, but it is clear that the replacement of Esquire by Mr. is gaining ground rapidly. In addressing a man abroad, unless you use M. (Monsieur) or Herr, Mr. will have to be used, as there is no equivalent outside the United Kingdom for Esquire.

Messrs.

Messrs. should not be used before the name of any limited company, even one containing persons' names, as the company has an identity distinct from that of its proprietors, the shareholders. It is, in fact, a 'thing'; for this reason to salute it as 'Dear Sirs' is illogical. The letter should be addressed to, for example, the Manager or to the General Manager, or, if appropriate, to the Secretary, when the salutation will be 'Dear Sir'.

Example: The General Manager,

       Smith Brown Jones & Co. Ltd.,

Messrs. must precede the name whenever it indicates that more than one person is involved, such as a firm of accountants or solicitors, or a small business concern.

Example: Messrs. A. Smith & Company

10

NUMBERS

Decimal Sign

The decimal sign is the point. For weights and measures, the point is placed on the line in printed, handwritten and typed material, e.g. 1.505 m.

Thousands Marker

The space is to be used as the thousands marker. Four figures or less may be blocked together, e.g.

1000 kg
1000 litres

Five or more are to be grouped in threes divided by single spaces, e.g.

10 000
1 000 000

But when tabulating numbers, all numbers should be grouped in threes to keep them in columns and to ensure clarity, e.g.

1 000
10 000
100 000
———
111 000
———

Note: the comma is still used for indicating thousands in currency.

11

PUNCTUATION

The modern tendency is to dispense with as much punctuation as possible. This is good, but if carried too far, it can lead to difficulty in interpreting the sense of what has been written. Aim at adopting a simple style and avoiding over-punctuation.

Comma

The comma is used to separate nouns, adjectives, phrases, etc., where there is a pause in the sentence. The comma is important and the most misused of punctuation signs. Many people find it impossible to use commas correctly. Remember that a comma marks the type of pause you would make in reading aloud.

Full Stop

The main use of the full stop is to mark the end of a sentence. It is also used to mark abbreviations.

Semicolon

The semicolon lies half-way between the comma and the full stop. It is used to divide two clauses which are too near to be separated into two sentences by a full stop, but need stronger punctuation than the comma. The semicolon, apart from literary compositions, should be used sparingly.

Colon

In modern usage the colon is used mainly to introduce lists, quotations, etc.

PRACTICAL TYPEWRITING

Inverted Commas

These are used to denote direct speech—the actual words used by a person.

Question Marks

These are used to show a direct question as distinct from an indirect—e.g. 'Are you going home?' and 'I want to know if you are going home'.

Use of Capital Letters

There is a tendency today to give capital letters to nouns that do not require them. The following information may help:

1. Use a capital letter for the first word of
   (*a*) a sentence;
   (*b*) a direct quotation;
   (*c*) a line of poetry.

2. Use a capital for all proper nouns.

12

PUNCTUATION RULES

Space once:

(*a*) after a comma;
(*b*) after a semicolon (also a colon, if you have decided to adopt this alternative);
(*c*) after the full stop in an abbreviation;
(*d*) between a whole number and a 'made' fraction;
(*e*) before and after the ampersand;
(*f*) before and after a dash.

Space twice:

(*a*) after the full stop at the end of a sentence;
(*b*) after a colon;
(*c*) after the exclamation mark.

Do not space:

(*a*) between parentheses and the words they enclose;
(*b*) between quotation marks and the words they enclose;
(*c*) before or after the hyphen in compound words;
(*d*) before or after a decimal point;
(*e*) before or after a comma in groups of figures;
(*f*) before or after the apostrophe;
(*g*) before the % symbol;
(*h*) before or after the full stop in the time of day.

13

REFERENCE BOOKS

Business

Bankers' Almanac and Year Book, published annually by Thomas Skinner Directories. Detailed information about financial institutions.

Directory of Directors, published annually by Thomas Skinner Directories.

Stock Exchange Official Year Book, published annually by the Stock Exchange. Information concerning all British companies quoted on the London Stock Exchange.

Central Government

Civil Service Year Book, published annually by HMSO. Functions of Government Departments, lists of Ministers and higher civil servants.

Local Government

Municipal Year Book, published annually by Municipal Journal Ltd. Lists of local authority councils and principal officers. Brief descriptions of services operated by each authority.

Parliament

Dod's Parliamentary Companion, published annually by Dod's Parliamentary Companion Ltd. Biographical details of members of both Houses. Glossary of Parliamentary procedures and terms.

Persons of Distinction

Titles and Forms of Address: A Guide to their Correct Use, Adam & Charles Black. Also contains a useful list of abbreviations and a guide to the correct pronunciation of some difficult surnames.

Debrett's Correct Form, Kelly's Directories. Similar information to that in *Titles and Forms of Address*.

Who's Who, published annually by Adam & Charles Black. Several thousand short biographies of notable persons.

Travel

A/ Street Atlas with A-Z index: London, Geographers' A-Z Map Co. Similar atlases are available for most towns and cities in the U.K.

ABC Railway Guide, published monthly by ABC Travel Guides.

ABC World Airways Guide, published by ABC Travel Guides.

For General Reference

A Dictionary of Foreign Words and Phrases in Current English, Routledge & Kegan Paul Ltd.

The Complete Plain Words (A guide to English Usage), HMSO.

Whitaker's Almanack, published annually by J. Whitaker & Sons Ltd. General information on many subjects. The index is at the front of each volume.

14

REPROGRAPHY (TYPING FOR DUPLICATION)

Various methods are used to produce copies of documents. They include ink duplicating, spirit duplicating, offset lithography duplicating and photocopying.

One of the important advantages of duplicating and offset-litho processes is that they are generally cheaper than printing. Only when several thousand copies of a document are wanted does printing become competitive. Printers' type is both expensive to set and to retain for subsequent use, whereas the stencils and plates used in duplicating and reprographic installations can be stored inexpensively for long periods.

Stencil Duplicating

One of the most economical methods of reproducing a large number of copies is by the use of stencils. The modern stencil can be stored and used many times. An ink duplicating machine is required. To produce a good stencil the typewriter should have good sharp type and the following routine should be observed:

1. The type faces should be clean and in good condition.
2. Disengage the ribbon by moving the ribbon switch to the stencil position.
3. Insert carbon paper, coated side to the stencil.
4. If using a manual typewriter, the typist should use a sharp, even touch. Any unevenness in striking the keys will show on the copies. If too heavy a touch is used, the centres of certain letters (o in particular) are likely to be cut out. If this happens the centre should be carefully replaced with a pin. If this is not done a black blob (instead of o) will appear on the copies.
5. When setting the margin stops, care should be taken to ensure that the type does not extend beyond the lines given for the size of paper required.
6. Errors are corrected with the special correcting fluid. Lightly paint out the letters with the fluid; when the fluid is dry retype over the letters painted out.

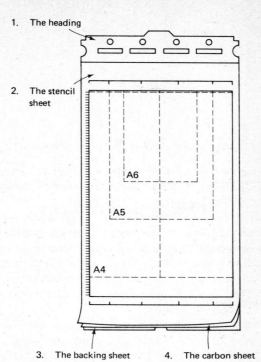

Fig. 10. A duplicating stencil.

Spirit Duplicating

With this type of reproduction a spirit-duplicating machine is necessary. The master is prepared from a special one-sided chromo paper, either written, drawn or typed. The master sheet is placed with the shiny side downwards on top of a special carbon, with the carbon coating face upwards. These special hectograph carbons can be used only once. Using a backing sheet, the two papers should be inserted into the typewriter and the master typed through the ribbon in the usual way on to the dull side of the paper.

Two hundred copies is generally considered to be the maximum obtainable from this method.

Points to observe when typing masters

1. Type faces should be clean and in good condition.
2. If using a manual typewriter, the typist should use a sharp, even touch.
3. Errors can be corrected by means of a spirit eraser or by scraping the carbon off the master with a sharp metal blade.

15

SOME SPELLING RULES

1. In words ending in a consonant preceded by a vowel, double the final consonant before adding 'ed', 'ing' and 'er'. Examples:

   sin, sinner
   run, running
   travel, travelled

   However, the consonant is not doubled when the stress is on the first syllable, as in: profit, profiting. (There are exceptions e.g. worship, worshipping.)

2. When a word begins with 's', the 's' is retained after adding 'mis' and 'dis' to the beginning of the word. Examples:

   spell, misspell
   solve, dissolve

3. Words ending in 'y' preceded by a consonant change to 'i' when a syllable is added. Examples:

   rely, relied
   fry, fried
   imply, implied

Plurals

Most plurals are formed by adding 's'. There are some words which can be treated as singular or plural, such as mumps, measles, innings, corps. In the word 'corps' the 's' is silent in the singular but sounded in the plural. An 'innings' and several 'innings' show

PRACTICAL TYPEWRITING

no distinction. The plural of 'penny' is 'pence', but when referring to the individual coins, the plural is 'pennies', e.g. 'only pennies will work this machine'.

Other plurals to watch are compound words such as 'court martial', which becomes 'courts martial', 'Lord Justice' which becomes 'Lords Justices', and 'mother-in-law', the plural of which is 'mothers-in-law'.

16

TYPEWRITING PAPER

For many years the most common sizes of paper used were:

>Quarto (8 × 10 inches)
>Octavo (8 × 5 inches)

Now an international standard size of paper has been introduced, the measurements of which are based on the metric system. The two sizes of paper most commonly used are:

>A4   210 mm × 297 mm (8.27 × 11.69 inches)
>A5   210 mm × 148 mm (8.27 × 5.84 inches)

A5 is exactly half the size of A4 paper and can be used with either the short or long dimension across the top ('portrait' and 'landscape').

Paper quantities

24 sheets = 1 quire
20 quires = 1 ream
480 sheets = 1 ream

17

TYPING SUMS OF MONEY

When typing sums of money, you should use either the pound sign or the pence sign, not both together. For example:

>   £25
>   £25.50
>   75p
>   52½p

For mixed amounts, use the £ sign only, e.g. £25.50; £27.29; £3.45.

For amounts under a pound, e.g. 97p, use the form '97p' for general use, and '£0.97' as a more formal expression.

The use of 'p' for amounts above £1 is incorrect—e.g. 105p should be typed as £1.05.

Two digits should always be used in the pence column. Such use will prevent confusion between, for example, 8p (£0.08) and 80p (£0.80).

18

WORDS AND FIGURES

Use words:

(a) For numbers one to nine inclusive.
(b) When the number is expressed in an indefinite manner, as: there were about three hundred people present.
(c) When a number commences a sentence.
(d) For ages, when expressed as ordinal numbers, e.g. he was in his twenty-third year.
(e) For the time of day, when 'o'clock' is used; figures should be employed with a.m. and p.m.
(f) In cheques, estimates, and in legal and other documents where it is essential to ensure accuracy or to prevent the possibility of fraudulent alterations, it is usual to type both figures and words.
(g) When referring to street names, such as 'Seventeenth Avenue', but if a word precedes the number it is optional whether it should be spelt out, as 'West Fifteenth Street' or 'West 15th Street'.

Use figures:

(a) When the sign % is used.
(b) For dates, scores, weights, measurements and numbers of houses in streets.

Note: Avoid mixing words and figures in the same sentence or phrase; type either 10,000 or ten thousand, but not 10 thousand.

19

WORD PROCESSORS

The simple type of word processor looks like a conventional typewriter, with a one-line screen display. The more sophisticated models have full-page display screen separate from the printer. This means that one text can be typed or edited on the screen while another is being printed out automatically on the printer. Printing is carried out at a speed of about 500 wpm.

Word processors can best be described as computerised typewriters. Typing is done in the normal way on a conventional typewriter keyboard, but the text appears not on paper, but on a screen called a visual display unit (VDU). If a mistake is made, the typist simply backspaces and retypes. Corrections can be made, and words, sentences or paragraphs can be added, deleted or moved.

The information fed into the machine is stored on a magnetic disc. These discs are similar in size and shape to a 45 rpm single record. The number of pages which can be stored on a disc varies according to the particular system used. A fairly sophisticated model will have a capacity of about 150 A4 pages. An index of its contents is kept with each disc.

Text recorded on the disc can be recalled for display on the screen or for printing out. The machine can be 'told' to move a paragraph from one part of the text to another and it will be done without the need for retyping. Alterations can be made to the text and only the part to be altered need be retyped. This saves time in checking since only those parts of the text which have been altered need be checked. Thereafter the work can be printed out as many times as required.

The advantages of word processors are that they relieve the typist from the tedium of retyping long documents to which some alterations are necessary. From the point of view of the employer, substantial savings can be made in the cost of producing typewritten work as the work is executed more quickly.

20

SHORTHAND

Having mastered the art of typing, you may wish to improve your skills by learning shorthand. A companion volume in this series, *Teeline Shorthand Made Simple*, by H. Butler, will enable you to master the simple and logical Teeline system in less time than traditional systems.

Teeline Shorthand Made Simple presents the entire system step by step with speed material as you progress. In addition to helping you master the shorthand system itself, the text gives guidance for bilingual secretaries, medical secretaries and journalists and for those who wish to teach the system to others.

Available from all good bookshops. In case of difficulty, write to:

Made Simple Books
William Heinemann Ltd.,
10 Upper Grosvenor Street,
London W1X 9PA